Illustrator:
Nicole Francine

Editor:
Mary Kaye Taggart

Editorial Project Manager:
Karen J. Goldfluss, M.S. Ed.

Editor in Chief:
Sharon Coan, M.S. Ed.

Art Director:
Elayne Roberts

Associate Designer:
Denise Bauer

Cover Artist:
Keith Vasconcelles

Product Manager:
Phil Garcia

Imaging:
Ralph Olmedo, Jr.
Alfred Lau
James Edward Grace

Publishers:
Rachelle Cracchiolo, M.S. Ed.
Mary Dupuy Smith, M.S. Ed.

Portfolios Through the Year

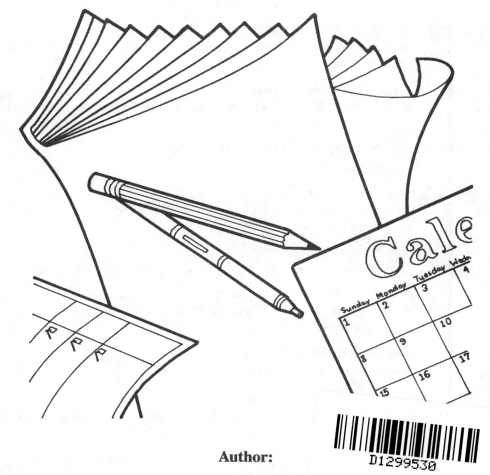

Author:

Carol French Cobb, M.A.

Teacher Created Materials, Inc.
P.O. Box 1040
Huntington Beach, CA 92647
ISBN-1-57690-036-3

©1996 Teacher Created Materials, Inc.   Made in U.S.A.

Table of Contents

Introduction

Why Portfolios?

Portfolios are more than folders of writing samples. They are organized collections, utilized by students and teachers in observing a student's growth in knowledge, ability, and attitudes. Portfolio assessment also serves as a method to monitor effort, improvement, and accomplishment.

The use of process writing resulting in high quality work improves attitudes toward writing for many students. The reflection, collection, and selection of material to go either into a quality work portfolio or to be retained in a working notebook helps students see for themselves what they must do to create quality work.

Why Use Rubrics and Grade Sheets Together?

Most school districts have encouraged the use of rubrics in essay writing but still require teachers to award letter grades on report cards responding to percentages the students receive on work. The combination of the two types of assessment help the students to see both methods of evaluation. Each unit has several criteria introduced with the assignment which enable all students to have a better chance to succeed in at least one area. This success creates the incentive to improve in the other areas.

Why Student Evaluation, Peer-Editing, and Peer-Conferencing?

Often, students will help their peers see content problems during the peer-conference times or mechanical errors during the peer-editing times more easily than a teacher who may not have the time for one-on-one conferences. The simple act of reading a writing piece aloud to a friend may be beneficial to the author.

Why Reflection?

We all need to take the time to evaluate our performances, but often we are pressed to go on to the next task and do not assess what we have just finished. The reflection for each unit will help your students see how much they have learned and check to confirm that they are not repeating their past mistakes.

Why Student Choice for Portfolio Selection?

Students who take an active role and ownership in their own learning will become stronger students. When students are allowed to choose which writing projects will be placed in their portfolios and which projects will remain in their working notebooks they will be recognizing their strengths and weaknesses.

Introduction *(cont.)*

Why Reassessment?

Reassessment is a very important aspect of the writing process. If a student wishes to create the very best quality work, he or she will need time to rewrite or complete a project. Establish a specified time limit within which students must complete their revisions. The final grades need to be averaged with the original teacher copy to give a balanced view of the improving writing process.

How to Use This Book

Portfolios Through the Year contains a variety of unit projects to be completed throughout the year. The finished projects will be included as part of each student's total portfolio package.

Each student will need the following materials:

- an eight-pocket folder for the year's portfolio
- a two-pocket folder for work in progess (This is called a Writer's Working Notebook. It is a great place to store brainstorming ideas, rhyming lists, and student skill lists.)

Throughout the units, each student will follow the process of brainstorming, writing a first draft, peer-conferencing for content, peer-editing for mechanical errors, followed by writing a second draft. The second drafts will then be submitted to the teacher for letter grades based on individual criteria and a rubric score. (Students should be apprised of the criteria and what will be expected of them when each assignment is given.) The teacher will then return the projects and the students will complete a final copy unless their second drafts were error-free. Finally, the students will fill out the accompanying reflection pages. At this point, the students will decide to file their projects in their portfolios for quality work or in their writer's notebooks for later reworking. The students may also rewrite their papers for reassessment.

The activities on pages 11 and 12 are designed to help students learn more about themselves. The unit on goal setting is a short project and is not necessarily graded by the teacher. Lesson plans for the teacher, a rubric, and a student grade sheet are provided in each unit.

Introduction *(cont.)*

How to Use This Book (cont.)

Rubrics and traditional grades are combined in these assessments because most school districts have not totally given up grades of A, B, C, D, and F, but are using rubrics, especially for writing assignments. The grade sheets include several criteria for each project. More than likely, each student will at least succeed in one area and this will provide an incentive to rework other areas of the project to a higher degree of quality.

In addition, student planning sheets which model the correct form of the particular genre are included. Peer-editing, peer-conferencing, and student self-evaluating sheets are also available. Although these sessions can be time-consuming, students will discover both content and mechanical errors which will ultimately save time for the teacher.

Each unit also provides rubric and grade sheets for the teacher to copy. Four grade sheets have been economically placed on each page. These small-size assessments may be attached to the papers before returning them to the students.

After completing their reflection cover sheets your students will decide if their works are worthy of being put into their portfolios or just in their working notebooks for future consideration. A reflection is always encouraged. If the student requests it, he or she may submit a work a second time to improve any one of the criteria areas.

This portfolio book contains the following:

- ❏ ideas for portfolio and writer's notebook set-up
- ❏ different genres of writing
- ❏ poetry units—cinquains and couplets
- ❏ fiction—plot, theme, and character development
- ❏ personal narrative/fiction—personification
- ❏ figures of speech—hyperbole, simile, metaphor
- ❏ student evaluations/reflections
- ❏ rubrics and grade sheets
- ❏ expository writing
- ❏ mini-lessons on writing leads and dialogue
- ❏ bibliography—suggestions of additional books on portfolios and writing
- ❏ resources for information

You may wish to punch holes in the pages of this book and store them in a three-ring binder to keep it intact.

Monthly Calendar Suggestions

The sample calendars on pages 6–10 show how to apply the activities in this book in a traditional school year.

September

Sunday	Monday	Tuesday	Wednesday	Thursday	Friday	Saturday
1	2 Labor Day No School	3 Fill out goals and seal in envelope	4 Learning Styles Questionnaire	5 Learning Styles Reflections	6	7
8	9 SMARTS paragraphs	10 SMARTS Peer Conferences	11	12	13 SMARTS final copy: display in bag	14
15	16 SMARTS final copy: display in bag	17	18 Patchwork Quilt Cover Peer-ed	19 Patchwork Quilt Cover Peer-ed	20 Patchwork Quilt due for laminating	21
22	23	24	25	26 Writer's Notebook Cover	27 Writer's Notebook Cover due	28
29	30 Writer's Notebook Cover due		Open days-grammar lessons	**Notes:** SMARTS great for Open House or Back-to-School Night.		

October

Sunday	Monday	Tuesday	Wednesday	Thursday	Friday	Saturday
		1 Resume Introduced	2 Resume peer-conf and peer-ed	3 Resume Draft due	4 Resume 2nd draft due to teacher	5
6	7 Autobio assigned Student Plan	8 Resume—Return to students	9 Reflect/ reassess resumes	10	11 Autobio peer-conf & peer-ed	12
13	14 Autobio 2nd draft due	15	16	17	18	19
20	21 Autobio returned to students	22 Autobio reflections or reassessments	23	24 Autobio reassessment due	25	26
27	28 Mark Twain Mysteries begin	29 Mystery Planning: Plot/Theme	30	31 Mystery Story sharing		

Monthly Calendar Suggestions *(cont.)*

November

Sunday	Monday	Tuesday	Wednesday	Thursday	Friday	Saturday
					1 Mystery—Metaphors and Similes	2
3	4 Mystery—peer-conference and peer-editing	5 Mystery—assign second draft	6 Mystery—second draft homework	7	8 Mystery—Cover Sheet in class	9
10	11 Mystery—second draft due	12	13 Mystery—About the Author	14	15	16
17	18 Mystery—return to students	19	20 Optional: work on computer	21 Work on computer	22	23
24	25 Work on computer	26 Work on computer	27 Cover, story, and author's page due	28	29	30

December

Sunday	Monday	Tuesday	Wednesday	Thursday	Friday	Saturday
1	2 Cinquain Poem—give assignment	3	4 Cinquain—peer-editing	5	6 Cinquain—second draft due	7
8	9 Cinquain—return to students	10 Cinquain—reflection	11	12 Cinquain—reassessment	13	14
15	16	17 Holiday Mouse Story	18 Personification mini-lesson	19 Mouse Story—draft due after holidays	20 Quotation mini-lessons	21
22	23 Usual Winter Holidays	24	25	26	27	28
29	30	31				

Monthly Calendar Suggestions *(cont.)*

January

Sunday	Monday	Tuesday	Wednesday	Thursday	Friday	Saturday
			1	2 Review Holiday Mouse Story	3 Review	4
5	6 Mouse Story—peer-conference	7	8	9 Mouse Story—second draft due	10	11
12	13	14	15 Mouse Story—return to students	16 Mouse Story—reflection	17	18
19	20 Mouse Story—reassessment	21	22	23	24	25
26	27	28	29	30	31	

February

Sunday	Monday	Tuesday	Wednesday	Thursday	Friday	Saturday
						1
2	3 Chocolate Poem—give assignment	4 Rhyming and rhythm mini-lesson	5	6 Chocolate Poem—peer-conference	7	8
9	10 Chocolate Poem—second draft due	11	12	13 Chocolate Poem—return to students	14 Chocolate Poem—reflection and reassessment	15
16	17 Chocolate Picture—workday	18 Chocolate Picture—peer-conference	19 Chocolate Poem—final draft due	20 Chocolate Picture—final draft due	21 Chocolate Picture—laminate pictures	22
23	24	25 Chocolate Picture—reflection	26	27	28	

Monthly Calendar Suggestions *(cont.)*

March

Sunday	Monday	Tuesday	Wednesday	Thursday	Friday	Saturday
						1
2	3 Persuasive Essay—introduce assignment	4 Essay—plan introductions	5 Essay—more planning	6 Essay—finish planning	7	8
9	10 Essay—peer-conference	11	12	13	14 Essay—second draft due	15
16	17	18	19	20 Essay—return to students	21 Persuasive Speech—introduce assignment	22
23 30	24 31	25	26 Essay—Final draft due	27	28 Essay—reflection	29

April

Sunday	Monday	Tuesday	Wednesday	Thursday	Friday	Saturday
	Allow extra time for spring break this month!	1 Speech—planning	2	3 Speech—rehearsals	4	5
6	7 Speech—rehearsals	8	9	10	11	12
13	14 Speech—presentations, audio/video taping	15 Speech—presentations, audio/video taping	16 Speech—presentations, audio/video taping	17 Speech—presentations, audio/video taping	18 Speech—presentations, audio/video taping	19
20	21 Speech—reflection	22	23	24	25	26
27	28	29	30			

Monthly Calendar Suggestions *(cont.)*

May

Sunday	Monday	Tuesday	Wednesday	Thursday	Friday	Saturday
				1	2	3
4	5 Plan portfolio presentations	6	7 Review inventory for year	8 Final portfolio reflection	9	10
11	12 Portfolio presentations	13 Committee presentation	14	15	16	17
18	19 Portfolio party for parents	20 Parent portfolio assessment	21 Portfolio party for another class	22	23	24
25	26	27	28	29 Students take home portfolios	30	31

Month _____

Sunday	Monday	Tuesday	Wednesday	Thursday	Friday	Saturday

Beginning-of-the-Year Questionnaire

Name: _____

Birth date: _____

Address: _____

_____

Parents' Names: _____

_____

Brothers: _____

_____

Sisters: _____

_____

Favorite activity outside school: _____

_____

Favorite school class: _____

Favorite school activity: _____

_____

Hobbies: _____

_____

_____

Sports involvement: _____

_____

Beginning-of-the-Year Questionnaire *(cont.)*

I am best at _____

_____.

I enjoy reading about _____

_____.

I enjoy writing about _____

_____.

Before I write I like to _____

_____.

I like to write _____stories the best.

My favorite place to write is _____.

I like to write (check one)

☐ on a computer.

☐ on paper with pencil or pen.

Tell why.

_____

This school year I would like to learn about_____

_____

_____

_____

_____

_____.

**Bring this paper to your first teacher conference and then place this
questionnaire in your writer's notebook.**

Goal Setting Form

Setting goals for this school year will help you to organize and focus on your work. Use this activity sheet to be specific about what you want to accomplish this year. (**Note:** Make two copies of this form. You will keep one in your Writer's Working Notebook and give one to your teacher.)

Example—Organization: "I will use a three-ring binder to help organize my homework papers."

Personal goals

Organization _____

Study time _____

Homework _____

Social goals

Friends_____

Parents/family _____

Teachers _____

Academic goals

Writing _____

Reading _____

Math _____

Handwriting _____

Spelling _____

Social Studies_____

Science _____

Physical Goals

Eating habits _____

Exercise _____

P.E. Class _____

To prepare copy for teacher: Complete the form. Lay your hand, with your fingers spread open, on the back of this paper. With your other hand draw around the shape of your entire hand. It will be fun to compare the size of your hand now with the size of your hand at the end of the school year. Neatly fold this sheet in thirds and place it in the envelope provided. On the front write your name clearly. You may wish to write "Do Not Disturb!" or "Keep Out!" on your envelope. Give this to your teacher. We will open the envelopes during the last week of school to see how well you kept your goals and to compare hand prints.

Lesson Plan: Learning Styles

Objectives   Students will complete the questionnaire as honestly as possible. (The first answer is usually the best.)

Students will circle all of the numbers at the bottom of the questionnaire.

Students will complete the reflection forms to determine the best way to utilize the information they learned about themselves.

Materials   copies of pages 15–18

Introduction   Begin with a demonstration of several types of learning styles. Ask your students to participate in a demonstration. Have the students learn the same information in different manners. For example, one student might simply read the materials, one student might chant it to a beat, and another student might make out flash cards to review information. Point out that people have different learning styles which work for them. Discuss several types of strategies and techniques for studying, using the visual, auditory, and kinesthetic learning styles.

Assessment   Students will be graded on three aspects of the learning styles questionnaire and reflection (pages 15–17).

    A. Completeness

    B. Writing of the reflection and evaluation of his or her learning styles

    C. Mechanics: capitalization, grammar, and punctuation

Rubric Scores: **3 = High pass**   **1 = Needs revision**

                         2 = Moderate pass   **0 = No response**

Learning Styles Rubric

3	Student responds to directions, writes at least three study methods, demonstrates good sentence structure, and shows good understanding of study techniques.
2	Student responds to directions, writes less than three study methods, demonstrates adequate sentence structure, and shows some understanding of study techniques.
1	Student may not follow directions, writes less than three study methods, demonstrates poor sentence structure, and shows little understanding of study techniques.
0	No response

Reassessment   Students will have the opportunity to rewrite projects if they wish to improve their grades in specific skill areas.

Learning Styles Questionnaire

Name_____

Check only those statements which describe your behavior. Be honest and answer with your first thought. Then circle the numbers at the bottom of the page.

- ☐ 1. I am very quiet. I do not volunteer answers often.
- ☐ 2. I love to talk a lot.
- ☐ 3. I move my body more than I talk.
- ☐ 4. I love to put together difficult puzzles.
- ☐ 5. I move a lot and I rarely sit still.
- ☐ 6. I remember jingles and television commercials.
- ☐ 7. I dress neatly and wearing color-coordinated clothing is important to me.
- ☐ 8. I usually touch things I see.
- ☐ 9. I notice details about the world.
- ☐ 10. I do not always worry about being messy, and my room is a mess.
- ☐ 11. I am distracted by background noises.
- ☐ 12. I have a vivid imagination.
- ☐ 13. When I am angry, I stomp and/or slam a door.
- ☐ 14. In my spare time, I would most of all like to watch television.
- ☐ 15. I can express my feelings.
- ☐ 16. In my spare time, I enjoy listening to the radio, record player, and/or tapes.
- ☐ 17. I try to touch and feel things I am learning about.
- ☐ 18. Even when I am upset, I do not tell anyone.
- ☐ 19. In my spare time, I prefer to be jumping, running, and/or wrestling.
- ☐ 20. I can put together projects without looking at the directions.
- ☐ 21. I like to solve problems by talking out loud.
- ☐ 22. I sound out new words and I am a good speller.
- ☐ 23. I think I have a fairly long attention span.
- ☐ 24. When I hear directions orally, I can follow them easily.

Circle the numbers you have checked above and write the totals for each group on the lines.

Group One	1	4	7	9	12	14	18	20 |_____
Group Two	2	6	11	15	16	21	22	24 |_____
Group Three	3	5	8	10	13	17	19	23 |_____

Now refer to the second and third pages for ideas on how to use the information you have just learned about yourself.

Learning Styles Reflection Sheet

Name_____

Group One numbers indicate a *visual* learning style (seeing). These students need to read over information, first looking at the headings in a written text. Visual learners like to study from their own notes.

Group Two numbers indicate an *auditory* learning style (hearing). These students might benefit from tape recording notes from class or tape recording parts of the textbook. Auditory learners enjoy studying with friends over the telephone or in person.

Group Three numbers indicate a *kinesthetic* learning style. (movement) Studying techniques for this type of learner might be making flash cards or inventing a game to play.

Fill out the section (A, B, or C) below which applies to you.

A. If you discovered, on the learning style quiz, that you circled more numbers in *one* particular group (by at least two), which group was it? _____
This means you are a (an) _____ learner.

B. If you had *two* groups which had about the same amount of numbers circled, it means you use a combination of styles to learn. Which groups had the most circles?
_____ This means I am a (an) _____
and a (an)_____ learner.

C. If you had about the same number of circles on all *three* different types of learning styles you are a (an) _____ ,
a (an)_____ , and
a (an)_____ learner.

Learning Styles Reflection Sheet *(cont.)*

Now that you know what kind of learner you are, use this information to help you with your school work. If you learn information in a way that works well with your learning style(s) you will probably be more successful. For example, if you are an auditory learner, it would help you if you made up a song or chant to memorize something.

Think of some learning techniques that are appropriate for you. Consider the ways in which you learn the best. Also, think about what types of studying you are willing to make a commitment to doing. List these study methods in the box below. If you need some ideas to get you started, read the information at the bottom of the page. However, you are also expected to come up with some of your own ideas.

This year I will use methods for studying which work with my learning style(s), including the following:

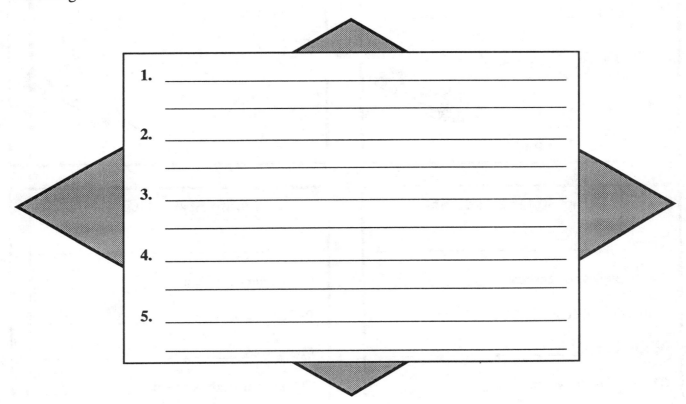

1. _____

2. _____

3. _____

4. _____

5. _____

Ideas for Study Strategies and Techniques for Each Learning Style

Visual Learners—reading notes and textbooks, taking notes, checking section headings

Auditory Learners—talking and listening to others such as studying with a friend, talking on the telephone about lessons, taping information and listening to the recording

Kinesthetic Learners—activities such as making and playing a game or studying with flash cards, making a model

Grade Sheets

Learning Styles Grade Sheet

Name _____

Completeness of answers _____

Reflection of styles _____

Mechanics _____

Thoughtful study strategies_____

Comments _____

_____

Rubric

Learning Styles Grade Sheet

Name _____

Completeness of answers _____

Reflection of styles _____

Mechanics _____

Thoughtful study strategies_____

Comments _____

_____

Rubric

Learning Styles Grade Sheet

Name _____

Completeness of answers _____

Reflection of styles _____

Mechanics _____

Thoughtful study strategies_____

Comments _____

_____

Rubric

Learning Styles Grade Sheet

Name _____

Completeness of answers _____

Reflection of styles _____

Mechanics _____

Thoughtful study strategies_____

Comments _____

_____

Rubric

Lesson Plan: Multiple Intelligences

Objectives   Students will write paragraphs of five or more sentences about their most prominent intelligence(s).

Students will support the intelligence(s) they are writing about with supporting ideas.

Students will refine the content and edit the mechanical errors of their paragraphs.

Students will prepare paragraphs for display on a bulletin board.

Materials   copies of pages 20–25

Directions   Direct your students to write a paragraph of five or more sentences about their strongest intelligence areas. A mini-lesson, reviewing topic sentences and good sentence structure might be helpful at this point.

Assessment   Students will be graded on three aspects of this activity.

    A. Completeness of paragraph and reflection

    B. Use of good sentence structure in paragraph

    C. Evidence of understanding of personal intelligences

Rubric Scores:	**3 = High pass**	**1 = Needs revision**
	2 = Moderate pass	**0 = No response**

Intelligences Rubric

3   Student writes a paragraph of five sentences or more, demonstrates good sentence structure, and shows good understanding of personal intelligences.

2   Student writes a paragraph of less than five sentences, demonstrates adequate sentence structure, and shows some understanding of personal intelligences.

1   Student writes a paragraph of less than three sentences, demonstrates poor sentence structure, and shows little understanding of personal intelligences.

0   No response

Reassessment   Students will have the opportunity to rewrite projects if they wish to improve their grades in specific skill areas.

Student Planner

Write a paragraph of at least five sentences, describing the type of intelligence in which you are especially strong. Give examples of activities you do to illustrate your strength in the particular intelligence area.

Example topic sentence: "Although I am good at many things, I think my strongest intelligence area is interpersonal for several reasons."

Seven Types of Intelligence ("Smarts")

1. **Verbal/Linguistic** (word smart)
   This type of person enjoys learning new words and writing.

2. **Visual/Spatial** (picture smart)
   This type of person likes to draw, sketch, paint, or design.

3. **Bodily/Kinesthetic** (body smart)
   This type of person is physically active and enjoys sports.

4. **Musical/Rhythmic** (music smart)
   This type of person likes to listen to music and may enjoy playing a musical instrument.

5. **Logical/Mathematical** (number and logic smart)
   This type of person likes to solve problems and puzzles.

6. **Interpersonal** (people smart)
   This type of person enjoys being social and being with a wide variety of people.

7. **Intrapersonal** (self smart)
   This type of person is usually confident and knows his or her strengths and what he or she wants in life.

Note: If you have more than one intelligence area that you consider your strongest, write your paragraph on both or all of these. Remember to use a broader topic sentence if you use two or more intelligence areas.

Before writing the first draft of your paragraph, ask yourself these questions:

a) Why am I smart in this area (or these areas)?

b) What are some examples which show that I am smart in this area (or these areas)?

c) Why is (are) this (these) intelligence(s) important to have?

Multiple Intelligences Student Forms

Checklist and Peer-Conferencing

I. Checklist

Look at the paragraph you wrote and check the following.

1. Did you indent?
   ❑ Yes   ❑ No

2. Did you stay within the margins?
   ❑ Yes   ❑ No

3. Read your paragraph to yourself. Have you left out any words? If you did, insert them now.

4. Did you have enough ideas to support the intelligence you selected?
   ❑ Yes   ❑ No

5. Write the first word in every sentence below. Then check the list for any repeating words. Did you start several sentences the same way? Change your paragraph so that each sentence starts in a different way.

   _____   _____   _____

   _____   _____   _____

6. Is your writing legible?
   ❑ Yes   ❑ No

II. Peer-Conferencing

Now, read your paragraph to another student, your peer-editor. Ask him or her to check "yes" or "no" after the questions below.

1. Did the author express his or her intelligence(s) clearly?
   ❑ Yes   ❑ No

2. Were there at least five sentences in the paragraph?
   ❑ Yes   ❑ No

3. Did the author use clear sentences without run-ons or sentence fragments?
   ❑ Yes   ❑ No

4. Did the author begin the sentences with a variety of words?
   ❑ Yes   ❑ No

Multiple Intelligences Student Forms *(cont.)*

Peer-Editing

III. Peer-Editing

Give your paragraph to your peer-editor. It is now the editor's responsibility to use a different colored pen to mark corrections directly onto the paper.

Note to the editor: Change grammar and punctuation errors with pen on the paper. However, if you think there is a spelling error, simply circle it. It is the author's responsibility to look up the word and correct the error.

1. Spelling errors?
   ❏ Yes ❏ No

2. Grammar errors?
   ❏ Yes ❏ No

3. Punctuation errors?
   ❏ Yes ❏ No

4. Capitalization errors?
   ❏ Yes ❏ No

5. Did the writer indent the paragraph?
   ❏ Yes ❏ No

6. Did the author follow the correct margins?
   ❏ Yes ❏ No

Editor's compliments about this project:_____

_____

_____

Editor's suggestions for improvement: _____

_____

_____

Multiple Intelligences Reflection Sheet

Name_____ Date _____

The intelligence area that I wrote about was _____ .

1. What writing skills did you learn while writing this paragraph?

   _____

   _____

   _____

2. Do you feel you selected your strongest intelligence(s) to write about? Why or why not?

   _____

   _____

   _____

3. If you were to write about your second strongest intelligence area, what would it be? Why?

   _____

   _____

   _____

4. What errors did your peer-conference and peer-editing partner help you find?

   _____

   _____

5. What areas of your paper were improved after the peer-conferencing and peer-editing?

   _____

   _____

6. Did you start your sentences in a variety of ways?

   _____

   _____

Verbal/Linguistic

Logical/Mathematical

Visual/Spatial

Bodily/Kinesthetic

Musical/Rhythmic

Interpersonal

Intrapersonal

Multiple Intelligences Reflection Sheet *(cont.)*

7. What would you improve in your paragraph if you had the opportunity to do it over?

_____

_____

_____

Now that you have spent some time examining your strong intelligences, ask yourself what intelligence areas you need to work on. Just because we do not have a natural strength in a certain area does not mean we cannot succeed in that area.

8. What is the intelligence area in which you are the weakest?

_____

What will you do to improve in this area during the school year? (Name at least two things.)

_____

_____

_____

9. What is a second intelligence area you would like to improve upon?

_____

What will you do to improve in this second intelligence area this school year? (Name at least two things.)

_____

_____

_____

_____

_____

Verbal/Linguistic

Logical/
Mathematical

Visual/Spatial

Bodily/Kinesthetic

Musical/Rhythmic

Interpersonal

Intrapersonal

Grade Sheets

Intelligences Grade Sheet

Name_____

Complete paragraph (five or more
sentences) _____

Sentence structure_____

Supporting ideas _____

Neatness/handwriting _____

Mechanics _____

Comments _____

_____

Rubric

Intelligences Grade Sheet

Name_____

Complete paragraph (five or more
sentences) _____

Sentence structure_____

Supporting ideas _____

Neatness/handwriting _____

Mechanics _____

Comments _____

_____

Rubric

Intelligences Grade Sheet

Name_____

Complete paragraph (five or more
sentences) _____

Sentence structure_____

Supporting ideas _____

Neatness/handwriting _____

Mechanics _____

Comments _____

_____

Rubric

Intelligences Grade Sheet

Name_____

Complete paragraph (five or more
sentences) _____

Sentence structure_____

Supporting ideas _____

Neatness/handwriting _____

Mechanics _____

Comments _____

_____

Rubric

Lesson Plan: Portfolio Patchwork Cover

Objectives   Students will design patchwork quilt covers with wrapping paper and magazine pictures.

Students will construct their quilt blocks with balance and neatness.

Students will represent aspects of their lives in a diverse manner.

Materials   pages 28–30 (two copies of each, reproduced onto construction paper—Cut one of each copy into pattern pieces.), magazines, wrapping paper, rubber cement or glue, scissors

Introduction   Lead a discussion about patchwork quilts and the history behind them. In the past, people reused old clothing to provide warmth and comfort in the interesting designs of quilts. Show an old quilt and discuss the fabric used to make it.

Directions   Direct students to decorate quilt patterns of their choice, using magazine pictures, wrapping paper, and the three patterns on the following pages. Staple the completed quilt covers to the fronts of the eight-pocket portfolio folders.

Assessment   Students will be graded on the following aspects of the cover:

A. Use of paper and magazine pages in creating a pattern

B. Neatness in cutting and gluing

C. Life represented in a balanced manner

Rubric Scores: 3 = High pass   1 = Needs revision

2 = Moderate pass   0 = No response

Portfolio Cover Rubric

3   Student responds to directions, uses paper and pictures to create a patterned portfolio cover, demonstrates aspects of his or her life through the use of magazine pictures, and shows neatness in cutting and gluing.

2   Student responds to directions, uses paper and pictures to create a patterned portfolio cover, demonstrates partial use of magazine pictures to show his or her life, and shows some neatness in cutting and gluing.

1   Student may not follow directions, presents an unclear and poorly balanced design for a portfolio cover, demonstrates poor use of a variety of magazine pictures to show his or her life, and shows little neatness in cutting and gluing.

0   No response

Reassessment   Students will have the opportunity to rewrite projects if they wish to improve their grades in specific skill areas.

Student Planner

Patchwork Quilt Portfolio Cover

Your assignment is to design a cover for your portfolio folder, using one of the three quilt blocks below.

Create patterns out of pieces of wrapping paper. For example, you may wish to cover every other small triangle in your block with red polka dotted paper and every square with blue striped paper. *You will be graded on the **balance of your design.***

Fill some of the shapes with pictures cut out of magazines. Search for pictures which tell something about your life, such as hobbies, pets, and places you have lived. *You will be graded on how well your cover **represents your life.***

Be sure to cut and glue neatly. Do not leave any part of the construction paper pattern showing. *You will be graded on **neatness.***

The three pattern choices vary in difficulty. You will receive five bonus points if you choose to do the Ohio Star and ten points for the Lemoyne Star, which is the most difficult.

Choose your pattern first, then plan the wrapping paper design first before placing magazine pictures. This will help you see the pattern first. Just shade in the areas where you want the paper.

Choose the patchwork quilt block you would like to use for your cover. Next, use the little version of your block (below) and crayons to decide where you will place your wrapping paper pieces. Color in a design to see how your plan might look.

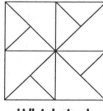

Whirlwind

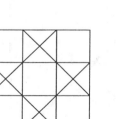

Ohio Star

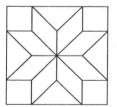

Lemoyne Star

Now start cutting out wrapping paper and magazine pictures for your cover pattern.

Whirlwind Pattern

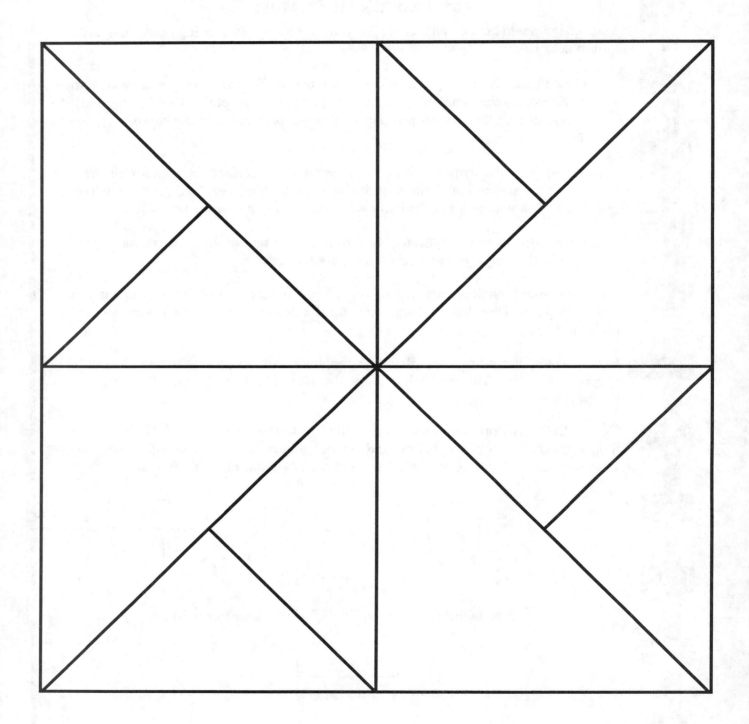

28

Lemoyne Star Pattern

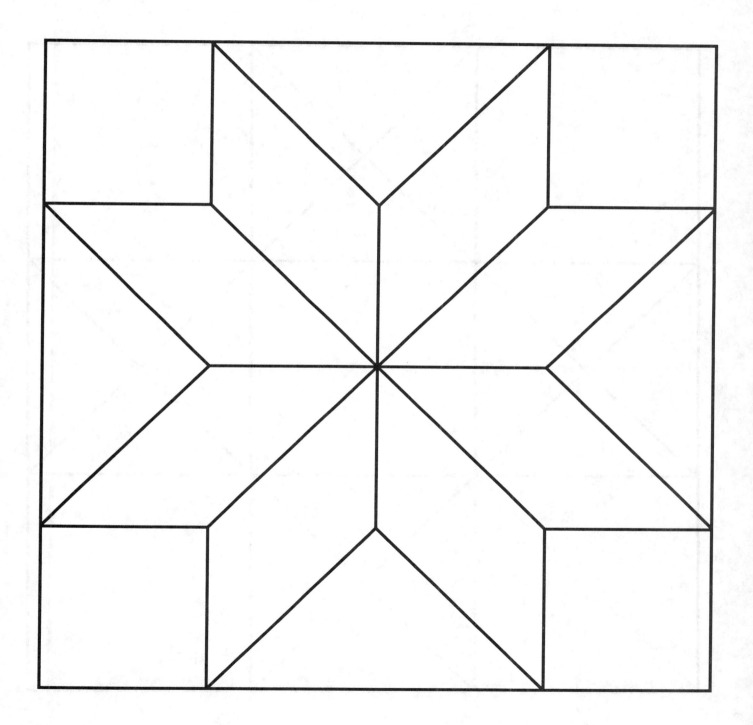

Ohio Star Pattern

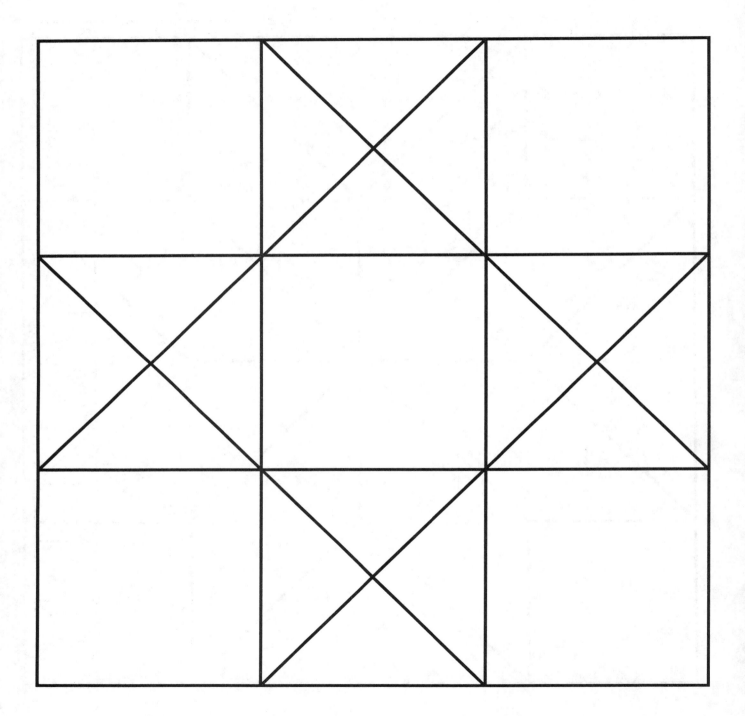

30

Portfolio Cover Reflection Sheet

Name_____ Date _____

1. How do you feel this cover reflects your favorite things and your personality?

   _____

   _____

   _____

   _____

2. How did you develop the basic pattern of your cover?

   _____

   _____

   _____

   _____

3. In what types of magazines did you find pictures about your life?

   _____

   _____

   _____

4. How did you use class time to work on this project? If you were talking with your friends, were you able to continue working at the same time?

   _____

   _____

   _____

Portfolio Cover Reflection Sheet *(cont.)*

5. Did you feel the need to rush through this project or did you have plenty of time?

_____

6. How would you do this project differently if you were to do it over?

_____

_____

_____

7. What part of the project did you like best and why?

_____

_____

_____

8. What do you believe was the purpose of this project?

_____

_____

_____

9. Give yourself a rubric score. (Circle one.)

   3 = High pass   **1 = Needs revision**

   2 = Moderate pass   **0 = No response**

Grade Sheets

Portfolio Cover Grade Sheet

Name _____

Balance of design _____

Representative magazine
pictures _____

Cutting and gluing
neatness _____

Comments _____

_____

Rubric

Portfolio Cover Grade Sheet

Name _____

Balance of design _____

Representative magazine
pictures _____

Cutting and gluing
neatness _____

Comments _____

_____

Rubric

Portfolio Cover Grade Sheet

Name _____

Balance of design _____

Representative magazine
pictures _____

Cutting and gluing
neatness _____

Comments _____

_____

Rubric

Portfolio Cover Grade Sheet

Name _____

Balance of design _____

Representative magazine
pictures _____

Cutting and gluing
neatness _____

Comments _____

_____

Rubric

Lesson Plan: Writer's Working Notebook

Objectives
Students will create notebook covers which reflect their personalities. The two-pocket folder will be a collection place for works in progress, uncompleted projects, and idea inventories.
Students will provide the information requested in the directions.
Students will use clear handwriting and colorful border decorations.

Materials
copies of pages 34 and 35, two-pocket folder, 8½" x 11" (22 cm x 28 cm) white construction paper (cut to fit the front of the two-pocket folder), markers or colored pencils, rubber cement, rulers

Introduction
Review with your students the three learning styles and the seven intelligences. Information from both of these lessons will be applied to the cover design activity. Lead a brainstorming session about the best ways to make an attractive cover. First, brainstorm about what types of lettering the students might want to use to write their names on the center of the cover. Second, encourage your students to brainstorm, on their own, a list of their favorite things. Ask them to consider the things they learned about themselves from the learning styles and seven intelligences lessons. Explain that they will need to choose one, some, or all of these favorite things to incorporate into a creative border for the front of their covers.

Directions
Direct your students to choose one or several of their favorite things and to creatively incorporate these things into a border. Ask them to plan, using their Student Planner, the cover design lightly in pencil before doing it in ink. Although there is no peer-conferencing and peer-editing sheets for this assignment, you may wish to recommend that your students share their projects with a friend before they begin to ink in their designs. The friends might identify messy areas, spelling errors, and places where the designs need improvement.

Assessment
Students will be graded on their ability to follow directions, write their names clearly, and creatively and neatly design and color the cover.

Rubric Scores:	3 = High pass	1 = Needs revision
	2 = Moderate pass	0 = No response

Learning Styles Rubric	
3	Student responds to directions, creates a cover which reflects his or her personality, demonstrates neatness.
2	Student responds to directions, creates a cover which only somewhat reflects his or her personality, demonstrates partial neatness, and project is only partially complete.
1	Student may not respond to directions, creates a cover unrelated to personality, demonstrates lack of neatness, and project is incomplete.
0	No response

Reassessment
Students will have the opportunity to rewrite their projects within three days if they wish to improve their grades in any specific areas.

Student Planner

All writers need a good place to keep their unfinished writing projects and brainstorming ideas. This two-pocket folder will be used to keep your notes and other helpful ideas, such as rhyming lists, editing symbols, vocabulary lists, and writing strategies. You may also use this folder to store drafts and writing projects that have not been completed to your satisfaction. Do not throw away works that you have written, but not completed. You never know if you may want to use these in the future as the beginnings of other great projects.

The cover for your folder will use the format shown in the examples below. Use the second page of this planner to brainstorm how your cover will appear.

Your strongest intelligence area   Your favorite color

Your first name

Your last name

Your learning style   Your favorite possession

Decorate a special border to reflect your interests.

Student Planner *(cont.)*

Before you make a cover for your folder, plan what you will be putting on it by answering the items below.

1. What is my strongest intelligence area? _____

2. What is my favorite color? _____

3. What is my learning style? _____

4. Brainstorm a list of your favorite things and then choose one to put on the cover of your folder.

   _____

   _____

5. Brainstorm a list of ideas for a border that would reflect your interests. Then choose one for your cover.

   _____

   _____

Now use the information above to create your folder cover. You will be graded on several aspects of this project.

> A. Following format and directions
> B. Clear writing of his or her name
> C. Design and color
> D. Neatness of design

Grade Sheets

Notebook Cover Grade Sheet

Name_____

Format followed _____

Name written clearly_____

Design and color_____

Neatness _____

Comments _____

_____

Rubric

Notebook Cover Grade Sheet

Name_____

Format followed _____

Name written clearly_____

Design and color_____

Neatness _____

Comments _____

_____

Rubric

Notebook Cover Grade Sheet

Name_____

Format followed _____

Name written clearly_____

Design and color_____

Neatness _____

Comments _____

_____

Rubric

Notebook Cover Grade Sheet

Name_____

Format followed _____

Name written clearly_____

Design and color_____

Neatness _____

Comments _____

_____

Rubric

Lesson Plan: Personal Resume

Objectives Students will fill out forms with informative phrases.

Students will fill out forms in neat printing.

Students will continue to refine and edit works based on peer-editing and peer-conferencing.

Students will complete a final resume in ink and without errors.

Materials copies of pages 39–45, pencils, erasable pens

Introduction Lead a discussion about the events in your students' lives that they feel are important to who they are and what they will do as adults. Then discuss what a resume is and the value of it in getting into college or getting a job. Share the examples on the student planning page. Which one is the best? What makes it a better resume?

Directions Direct your students to fill out the resume first draft form in clear, printed phrases (not necessarily complete sentences). Explain that the reason resumes almost always ask for printing or typing is so that they can be read easily. Next, ask them to peer-conference and peer-edit to find errors in the first draft resumes. Students will then make a final resume copy to turn in to the teacher.

Assessment Students will be graded on three aspects of their resumes.

  A. Completeness of resume

  B. Neatness of writing

  C. Mechanics: capitalization, grammar, and punctuation

Rubric Scores: 3 = High pass   1 = Needs revision

        2 = Moderate pass 0 = No response

Learning Styles Rubric

3 Student responds to directions, completes resume, demonstrates neatness in printing, and uses mastery of mechanics and grammar.

2 Student responds to directions, partially completes resume, demonstrates partial neatness in printing, and uses partial mastery of mechanics.

1 Student may not respond to directions, uses unclear answers, demonstrates lack of neatness, and does not complete project

0 No response

Reassessment Students will have the opportunity to rewrite their projects if they wish to improve their grades in specific criteria areas.

Student Planner

Your assignment is to fill out the first draft of your resume as completely as possible. Most people need to use resumes to get jobs and to get into college. Resumes give a general picture of a person in a short space. These types of forms are usually typed or hand printed so that the employer, or anyone else who requests such forms, can read them easily. Please print your first and final drafts.

The second draft will be completed after the peer-conferencing and peer-editing sessions. You will be able to correct your errors and improve your answers.

You will be graded on three aspects of the resume: **completeness of resume, neatness of writing, mechanics (capitalization, grammar, and punctuation.)**

Look at the two examples of partial resumes. Which one is better? Why?

Example One

Name __Susan Parker__

Address __720__ __Grandview Drive__
(number) (street)

__St. Louis   MO__   __63131__
(city, state)   (zip code)

Telephone number __(314)   966-5888__

Background: Birth date __November 29, 1984__
(month, date, year)

Parents' names __Pat Parker__   __John Parker__
(mother)   (father)

Example Two

Name __Susan   Parker__

Address __722   Grandview Dr.__
(number) (street)

__St louis   Mo__
(city, state)   (zip code)

Telephone number __966-5888__

Background: Birth date __Nov   29   1984__
(month, date, year)

Parents' names __Pat Parker__   __John Parker__
(mother)   (father)

Personal Resume

Name: _____

Address: _____
       (number)   (street)

_____
  (city, state)   (zip code)

Telephone number: _____

Background

Birth date: _____ Birth location: _____
     (month) (date, year)   (city, state)

Parents' names: _____
                             (mother)

                _____
                             (father)

                _____
                          (stepparents)

Maternal grandparents: _____
(mother's parents)

_____

Paternal grandparents: _____
(father's parents)

_____

Preschool attended: _____

Elementary school(s) attended: _____

Work experience: _____

_____

_____

_____

_____

_____

Personal Resume *(cont.)*

Sports involvement: _____

Club membership(s): _____

Honors: _____

References

Name three people (not relatives) who can testify as to your good character.

(For example, former teachers or neighbors.)

1. _____

2. _____

3. _____

Hobbies

List three activities you do just for fun and relaxation.

1. _____

2. _____

3. _____

Life Goals

Career: _____

Personal: _____

Physical: _____

Your best signature: _____

Personal Resume Student Forms
Checklist and Peer-Conferencing

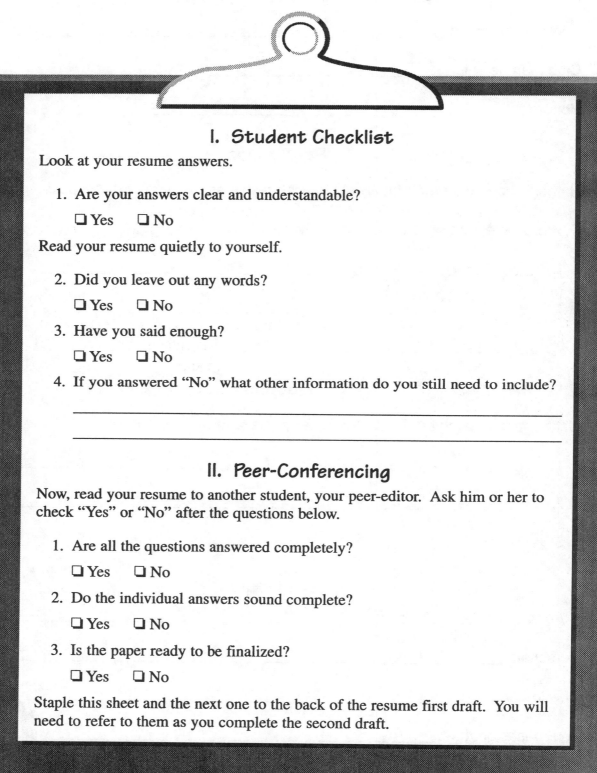

I. Student Checklist

Look at your resume answers.

1. Are your answers clear and understandable?
   ❑ Yes   ❑ No

Read your resume quietly to yourself.

2. Did you leave out any words?
   ❑ Yes   ❑ No

3. Have you said enough?
   ❑ Yes   ❑ No

4. If you answered "No" what other information do you still need to include?

   _____

   _____

II. Peer-Conferencing

Now, read your resume to another student, your peer-editor. Ask him or her to check "Yes" or "No" after the questions below.

1. Are all the questions answered completely?
   ❑ Yes   ❑ No

2. Do the individual answers sound complete?
   ❑ Yes   ❑ No

3. Is the paper ready to be finalized?
   ❑ Yes   ❑ No

Staple this sheet and the next one to the back of the resume first draft. You will need to refer to them as you complete the second draft.

Personal Resume Student Forms *(cont.)*
Peer-Editing

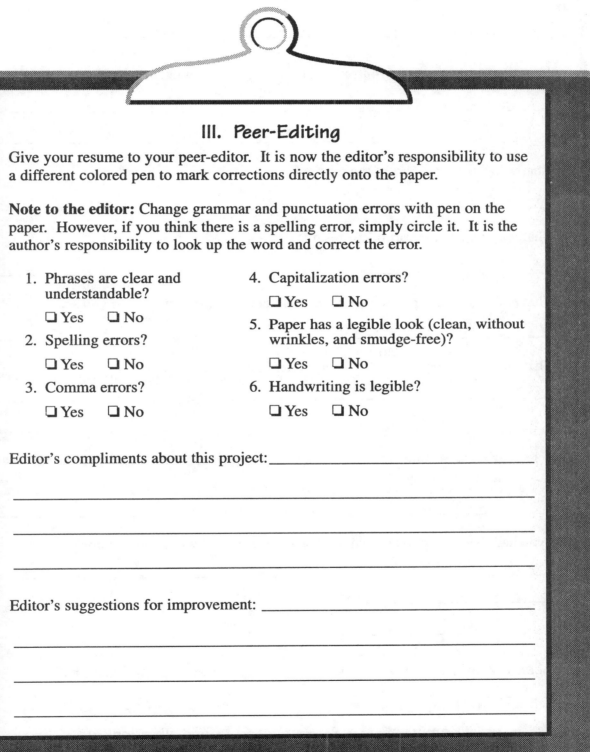

III. Peer-Editing

Give your resume to your peer-editor. It is now the editor's responsibility to use a different colored pen to mark corrections directly onto the paper.

Note to the editor: Change grammar and punctuation errors with pen on the paper. However, if you think there is a spelling error, simply circle it. It is the author's responsibility to look up the word and correct the error.

1. Phrases are clear and understandable?

    ❏ Yes   ❏ No

2. Spelling errors?

    ❏ Yes   ❏ No

3. Comma errors?

    ❏ Yes   ❏ No

4. Capitalization errors?

    ❏ Yes   ❏ No

5. Paper has a legible look (clean, without wrinkles, and smudge-free)?

    ❏ Yes   ❏ No

6. Handwriting is legible?

    ❏ Yes   ❏ No

Editor's compliments about this project: _____

_____

_____

_____

Editor's suggestions for improvement: _____

_____

_____

_____

Personal Resume Reflection Sheet

Name _____ Date _____

What did you learn about yourself while writing this resume?

_____

_____

What was the easiest part of the resume?

_____

What was the hardest part of the resume?

_____

What errors did your peer-conferencing and peer-editing partner help you see?

_____

What areas were improved after peer-conferencing and peer-editing?

_____

_____

Were your answers complete? Did you ask questions at home to help you fill out the questionnaire completely?

_____

If you had the chance to redo your resume, what would you improve upon?

_____

_____

_____

Check the areas below that were improved upon in your final draft.

❏ **Punctuation**   ❏ **Complete phrases**

❏ **Commas**   ❏ **Capitalization**

❏ **Spelling**   ❏ **Handwriting/printing**

Grade Sheets

Personal Resume Grade Sheet

Name _____

Completeness of answers _____

Neatness of printing _____

Mechanics _____

Comments _____

_____

Rubric

Personal Resume Grade Sheet

Name _____

Completeness of answers _____

Neatness of printing _____

Mechanics _____

Comments _____

_____

Rubric

Personal Resume Grade Sheet

Name _____

Completeness of answers _____

Neatness of printing _____

Mechanics _____

Comments _____

_____

Rubric

Personal Resume Grade Sheet

Name _____

Completeness of answers _____

Neatness of printing _____

Mechanics _____

Comments _____

_____

Rubric

Lesson Plan: Autobiography

Source of Activity This assignment is an extension of the Portfolio Patchwork Cover lesson and it is the completion of that project. This will be the first portfolio essay assigned for the year. It is designed to help you and your students learn more about each other. The assignment is designed to include five paragraphs. Each paragraph will specifically cover a special part of the students' lives. In the final paragraph, students will make an analogy between their lives and patchwork quilts.

Objectives Students will write a five paragraph essay about their lives.

Students will discuss these five areas: my life in general, personal description (appearance and personality), activities I am involved in, my hobbies, an analogy between my life and a patchwork quilt.

Materials copies of pages 47–53, paper, pens or pencils

Introduction Lead a discussion about comparing the designs and fabrics of patchwork quilts with the areas of our lives. Several different analogies may be discussed.

Directions Direct your students to brainstorm ideas about their lives before they begin writing, using the planning pages.

Assessment Students will be graded on three aspects of this project.

    A. Completeness of planner and reflection pages

    B. Content of five paragraph essay

    C. Mechanics of essay: capitalization, grammar, and punctuation

Rubric Scores: **3 = High pass**   **1 = Needs revision**

                        2 = Moderate pass   **0 = No response**

Autobiography Rubric

3	Student responds to directions, writes a five-paragraph essay about his or her life, demonstrates correct paragraph construction, uses mastery of mechanics, grammar, usage, and spelling.
2	Student responds to directions, writes a shorter essay about his or her life (less than five paragraphs), demonstrates partial understanding of paragraph construction, shows some mastery of mechanics.
1	Student may respond to directions, writes unclear thoughts about his or her life in a poorly organized essay, demonstrates a lack of understanding sentence and paragraph construction, uses mechanics that inhibits the reader's understanding.
0	No response

Reassessment Students will have the opportunity to rewrite their projects within three days if they wish to improve their grades in any criteria areas of the project.

Student Planner

Use the guidelines below to plan what you will write for the introduction and conclusion of your autobiography.

Paragraph One: Introduction

1. Write a quote, question, or attention-grabbing statement about you. Write a brief sentence about the events around your birth, the way you got a nickname, or a funny story.

2. Introduce yourself with your name, age, and where you live.

3. Write a physical description of yourself.

4. Present a transition sentence (for example, about how your life has been shaped by many people and activities).

Paragraph Five: Conclusion

1. Restate that your family, activities, and hobbies all make up who you are.

2. Mention any additional facts or ideas that make you special.

3. Compare a patchwork quilt to your life (analogy). You could compare the different colors and patterns to the different people and activities in your life. The solid-colored shapes might represent the calm times in your life, while the design fabric might represent the busy days of your life. What holds the quilt together? What holds your life together?

4. How do you feel about your life so far?

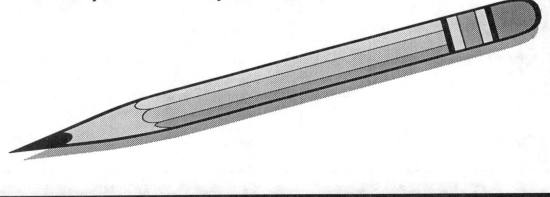

Student Planner *(cont.)*

In the chart below, write your ideas for paragraphs two through four.

Paragraph Two	Paragraph Three	Paragraph Four
Family names:	Activities:	Hobbies or special interests:
Short descriptions of your family members:	Stories about activities or specific events:	What you get out of hobbies:
How your family is important to you:	Why these activities are important to you:	Special things you learn with hobbies:

Autobiography Student Forms
Checklist and Peer-Conferencing

I. Checklist

1. Look at your autobiography. Do you have five paragraphs in your autobiography?
   ❏ Yes   ❏ No

Read your autobiography over quietly to yourself.

2. Have you left out any words?
   ❏ Yes   ❏ No

3. Have you said enough?
   ❏ Yes   ❏ No

4. If you answered "No," what other information do you still need to include?

   _____

   _____

II. Peer-Conferencing

Now, read your autobiography to another student, your peer-editor. Ask him or her to check "Yes" or "No" after the questions below.

1. Is the autobiography complete (five paragraphs)?
   ❏ Yes   ❏ No

2. Are paragraphs two, three, and four complete enough?
   ❏ Yes   ❏ No

3. Is the analogy appropriate?
   ❏ Yes   ❏ No

4. What did the writer compare the patchwork quilt to in his or her life?

   _____

   _____

Staple this sheet and the next one to the back of your autobiography first draft. You will need to refer to them as you complete your final draft.

Autobiography Student Forms *(cont.)*

III. Peer-Editing

Give your autobiography to your peer-editor. It is now the editor's responsibility to use a different colored pen to mark corrections directly onto the paper.

Note to the editor: Change grammar and punctuation errors with pen on the paper. However, if you think there is a spelling error, simply circle it. It is the author's responsibility to look up the word and correct the error.

1. Paragraphs are clear and understandable?
   ❑ Yes ❑ No

2. Spelling errors?
   ❑ Yes ❑ No

3. Punctuation errors?
   ❑ Yes ❑ No

4. Capitalization errors?
   ❑ Yes ❑ No

5. Paper has a legible look (clean, without wrinkles, and smudge-free)?
   ❑ Yes ❑ No

6. Handwriting is legible?
   ❑ Yes ❑ No

Editor's compliments about this project:_____

_____

_____

_____

_____

Editor's suggestions for improvement: _____

_____

_____

_____

_____

Autobiography Reflection Sheet

Name_____ Date _____

1. What skills did you learn while writing your autobiography?

   _____

   _____

   _____

2. What was the hardest part of writing the autobiography?

   _____

3. What was your favorite part of your autobiography?

   _____

4. Did you write enough about your family members?____If your answer is no, what should you have included?

   _____

   _____

   _____

5. Did you begin with a strong introductory paragraph? What made it strong or weak?

   _____

   _____

   _____

6. Did you use a strong, vivid vocabulary? What are some of the vocabulary words you used which helped make your paper stronger?

   _____   _____

   _____   _____

   _____   _____

   _____   _____

Autobiography Reflection Sheet *(cont.)*

7. What would you do to improve your autobiography if you had the opportunity to rewrite it?

_____

_____

_____

8. What areas of your paper were improved upon after reading your autobiography to a friend?

_____

_____

_____

9. Did you feel the need to rush through this project or did you have plenty of time?

_____

10. What do you believe was the purpose of this activity?

_____

_____

_____

_____

11. Will this piece of writing be placed in your portfolio or placed in your writer's notebook? Why?

_____

_____

_____

_____

_____

Place these reflection sheets with the final copy of your autobiography in either your portfolio folder or your working folder. Place it in the portfolio if you are pleased with the quality or in the working folder if you feel it needs improvement and does not reflect your best work.

Grade Sheets

Autobiography Grade Sheet

Name _____

Content/information _____

Sentence structure _____

Mechanics _____

Analogy _____

Comments _____

_____

Rubric

Autobiography Grade Sheet

Name _____

Content/information _____

Sentence structure _____

Mechanics _____

Analogy _____

Comments _____

_____

Rubric

Autobiography Grade Sheet

Name _____

Content/information _____

Sentence structure _____

Mechanics _____

Analogy _____

Comments _____

_____

Rubric

Autobiography Grade Sheet

Name _____

Content/information _____

Sentence structure _____

Mechanics _____

Analogy _____

Comments _____

_____

Rubric

Lesson Plan: Mark Twain Mystery

Objectives
Students will each write a short story (fiction), using four objects and at least three characters.
Students will plan the plot, theme, and setting before writing the stories.
Students will each use one metaphor and one simile within the text of the stories.
Students will create covers by computer or by hand. Each cover will include the title of story, the author's name, and a photo or picture to illustrate the title of the story.
Students will design back covers with photos (or self-drawn portraits) of the authors (themselves). They will also write short summaries of authors' lives.

Materials
pages 55–62, a list of objects to be used in writing the mystery (choose one from below):
1. A wooden music box playing *The Vienna Waltz,* a cameo pin, a corn cob pipe, and a broken toy telephone.
2. A feather boa, a brass candlestick, a gold pocket watch with the initials R. Z., and an unsigned letter.
3. A cuckoo clock, a gasoline can lid, a golden locket on a velvet ribbon, and an oval, cracked mirror.

Introduction
Tell your students that Samuel Clemens (Mark Twain) used to enjoy spinning bedtime stories for his daughters. The girls would collect objects to use in a story and then Mr. Clemens would create a story, using the objects in the order they were given to him.

Directions
Direct your students to use the planner to brainstorm ideas about plots and themes which can be used to write a story about a list of objects.

Assessment
Students will be graded on four aspects of the mystery story.
   A. Content of story
   B. Plot strength
   C. Mechanics
   D. Use of figures of speech (metaphor and simile)

Rubric Scores: 3 = High pass   1 = Needs revision
                      2 = Moderate pass   0 = No response

Mystery Rubric	
3	Student responds to directions, creates a fictional story with four objects, demonstrates understanding of plot, correctly uses metaphors and similes.
2	Student responds to directions, creates a fictional story with some of the objects, demonstrates understanding of plot, uses only one of the requested figures of speech (metaphors and similes).
1	Student may not respond to directions, creates a fictional story with only a few objects, demonstrates little understanding of plot in the story, uses mechanics that hinder the understanding of the story.
0	No response

Reassessment
Students will have the opportunity to rewrite their projects if they wish to improve their grades in any of the specific areas of assessment.

Student Planner

One of the greatest American writers of all time, Samuel Clemens, better known as Mark Twain, created mystery stories for his two daughters, Suzy and Clara. Every night Suzy and Clara would place a set of objects on the mantle in their bedroom. They would then ask their father to tell stories based on the objects and they insisted that the story should follow the same order that the objects were in. In this project you will have the opportunity to create a story the same way that Mr. Clemens did.

Choose a group of objects below and write a mystery story based on them. Be sure that you do not change the order of your set of objects in your story.

1. A wooden music box playing *The Vienna Waltz*, a cameo pin, a corn cob pipe, and a broken toy telephone.
2. A feather boa, a brass candlestick, a gold pocket watch with the initials R. Z., and an unsigned letter.
3. A cuckoo clock, a gasoline can lid, a golden locket on a velvet ribbon, and an oval, cracked mirror.

You will be graded on four parts of this assignment. They are content of story, plot strength, mechanics, and use of figures of speech (metaphor and simile). You will be given the opportunity for peer-conferencing and peer-editing. After examining your mistakes, you will write a high quality final draft.

Planning Form

Name _____ Date _____

Setting _____
        (Time)   (Place)

Characters: Major _____   Major _____

                 Major _____   Major _____

                 Minor _____   Minor _____

Theme (for example, robbery, missing person, lost treasure, "who done it?")

_____

Plot Line

Beginning (incorporate first object here) _____

Middle (incorporate second object here) _____

Climax (incorporate third object here) _____

Conclusion (incorporate fourth object here) _____

Student Planner *(cont.)*
Metaphors and Similes

After you have completed the first draft of the mystery and before the peer-conferencing and peer-editing session, look over your story for two places to insert a metaphor and a simile. Using these types of figures of speech will help make your writing more interesting.

A metaphor is a figure of speech that is used to describe someone or something by comparing it to something else. The use of a metaphor helps give a clearer picture of what is being described. This figure of speech usually has a linking verb. A metaphor does NOT use "as" or "like."

The masked man was a monster.
The fog was a whisper in the night.

To write the metaphor for your mystery, think of a noun already in your story. Then think of an unlike object. Combine these with a linking verb.

Noun	Linking Verb	Noun
_____	_____	_____

A simile is a figure of speech that compares two unlike things. The description includes "like" or "as."

The robber was as quiet as a cat.
The woman's eyes were like diamonds.

To write a simile for your mystery, think of a noun already in the story. Then think of another object. Link these with the words "as" or "like."

Noun	Comparison word (as or like)	Another Noun
_____	_____	_____

- - - - - - - - - - (Cut here and turn in the bottom portion to your teacher.) - - - - - - - -

Name: _____   Title of Mystery: _____

Metaphor: _____

_____

(This will be inserted into my mystery on page _____ .)

Simile: _____

_____

(This will be inserted into my mystery on page _____ .)

Story Cover Sheet (Front)

Title of Mystery

Story Illustration

Author's Name

Story Cover Sheet (Back)

About the Author

Drawing or Photograph of the Author

Summary of the Author's Life

_____

_____

_____

_____

_____

_____

_____

Mark Twain Mystery Student Forms
Checklist and Peer-Conferencing

I. Checklist

1. Look at your mystery story. Is it written in the correct form?
   ❏ Yes   ❏ No

2. Read your mystery to yourself quietly. Have you left out any words?
   ❏ Yes   ❏ No

3. Does it make sense?
   ❏ Yes   ❏ No

4. Have you said enough?
   ❏ Yes   ❏ No

5. If you answered "No" what other information do you still need to include about the characters, plot, or theme? _____

_____

II. Peer-Conferencing

Now, read your mystery to another student, your peer-editor. Ask him or her to check "Yes" or "No" after the questions below.

1. Is the story complete?
   ❏ Yes   ❏ No

2. Are the objects written into the story?
   ❏ Yes   ❏ No

3. Are the characters well described?
   ❏ Yes   ❏ No

4. Are the descriptions creative and appropriate?
   ❏ Yes   ❏ No

5. Does the story have clear setting and place?
   ❏ Yes   ❏ No

6. Does the story have a logical and understandable ending?
   ❏ Yes   ❏ No

7. Does the author start a new paragraph with each new time, place, and speaker?
   ❏ Yes   ❏ No

8. Do you understand the writer's metaphor?
   ❏ Yes   ❏ No

9. Do you understand the writer's simile?
   ❏ Yes   ❏ No

Attach this sheet and the next one to your first draft. You will need to refer to them as you complete your final draft.

Mark Twain Mystery Student Forms *(cont.)*
Peer-Editing

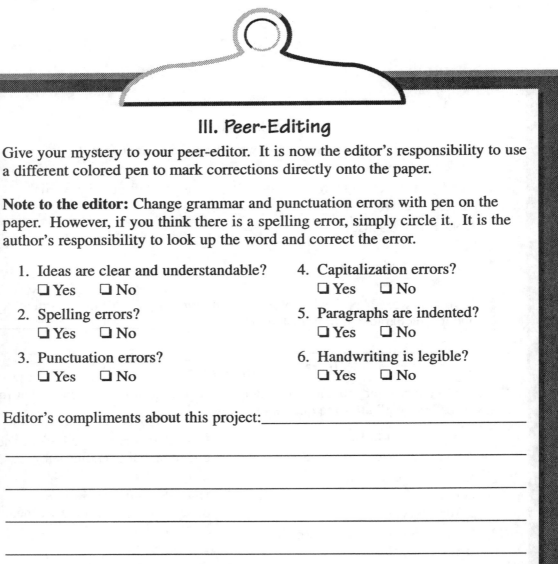

III. Peer-Editing

Give your mystery to your peer-editor. It is now the editor's responsibility to use a different colored pen to mark corrections directly onto the paper.

Note to the editor: Change grammar and punctuation errors with pen on the paper. However, if you think there is a spelling error, simply circle it. It is the author's responsibility to look up the word and correct the error.

1. Ideas are clear and understandable?
   ❏ Yes   ❏ No

2. Spelling errors?
   ❏ Yes   ❏ No

3. Punctuation errors?
   ❏ Yes   ❏ No

4. Capitalization errors?
   ❏ Yes   ❏ No

5. Paragraphs are indented?
   ❏ Yes   ❏ No

6. Handwriting is legible?
   ❏ Yes   ❏ No

Editor's compliments about this project:_____

_____

_____

_____

_____

Editor's suggestions for improvement: _____

_____

_____

_____

_____

Mark Twain Mystery Reflection Sheet

1. What skills did you learn while writing your mystery?

   _____

   _____

2. Give a brief summary of your plot.

   _____

   _____

3. What was the overall theme of your story?

   _____

   _____

4. What was the simile you wrote? _____

   What did it mean? _____

5. What was the metaphor you wrote? _____

   What did it mean? _____

   _____

6. Describe your front and back covers. Did you use color, and did you print neatly?

   _____

   _____

7. If you had the opportunity to rewrite your story, what would you improve upon?

   _____

   _____

8. What was your favorite part about writing your mystery?

   _____

   _____

9. What was the hardest part about writing your mystery?

   _____

   _____

Grade Sheets

Mystery Grade Sheet

Name_____

Content of story _____

Strength of plot_____

Use of theme_____

Metaphor_____

Simile _____

Mechanics_____

Comments_____

_____

Rubric

Mystery Grade Sheet

Name_____

Content of story _____

Strength of plot_____

Use of theme_____

Metaphor_____

Simile _____

Mechanics_____

Comments_____

_____

Rubric

Mystery Grade Sheet

Name_____

Content of story _____

Strength of plot_____

Use of theme_____

Metaphor_____

Simile _____

Mechanics_____

Comments_____

_____

Rubric

Mystery Grade Sheet

Name_____

Content of story _____

Strength of plot_____

Use of theme_____

Metaphor_____

Simile _____

Mechanics_____

Comments_____

_____

Rubric

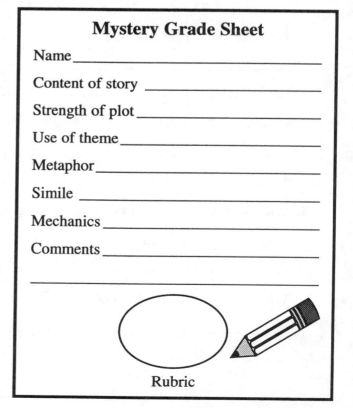

Lesson Plan: Cinquain Poetry

Objectives   Students will write five-line cinquain poems about nature.

Students will follow the directions for the grammar of each line.

Students will use effective synonyms.

Materials   copies of pages 64–68

Introduction   Lead a discussion about cinquain poetry and its basic rules. Hold a brainstorming session to develop a list of nature themes. If your students are having a difficult time thinking of themes, try holding your brainstorming session outside. Being outdoors should inspire more ideas and add to the excitement of this activity.

Directions   Direct your students to complete their Student Planners before writing their poems.

Assessment   Students will be graded on five aspects of their cinquain poems.

    A. Ideas of nature: content
    B. Use of adjectives
    C. Use of participles
    D. Mechanics
    E. Correct use of synonyms

Rubric Scores: **3 = High pass**   **1 = Needs revision**

    2 = Moderate pass   **0 = No response**

Cinquain Poem Rubric

3	Student responds to prompt, writes a five-line cinquain about nature, demonstrates correct use of grammar terms, shows a mastery of mechanics and spelling.
2	Student responds to prompt, writes less than a five-line cinquain about nature, demonstrates partial understanding of grammar terms, uses mechanics which enable the reader to understand.
1	Student may not respond to prompt, writes unclear thoughts about nature in the cinquain, demonstrates lack of understanding of mechanics and spelling, uses mechanics which inhibit the reader's understanding.
0	No response

Reassessment   Students will have the opportunity to rewrite their projects if they wish to improve their grades in any of the specific areas of assessment.

Student Planner

Cinquain poetry is often written about nature. Pick a nature topic and then brainstorm words associated with your topic.

Brainstorm Nature Topics:

(These are usually nouns such as *weather, wind, earth, sky, air,* or *birds*.)

_____

_____

Circle the topic you are going to write about.

Brainstorm Words About Your Topic:

What are some words you would use to describe your topic (adjectives)? _____

_____

List some -ing words about your topic (participles). _____

_____

Write a phrase or sentence, including a verb, about your topic. _____

_____

Write a one-syllable or one-word synonym for your topic. Your may use a different form of your topic (example: if your topic is *tree*, your ending synonym might be *oak*).

_____

Now refine the information above to create your poem. Follow the poetry form below. Pay special attention to the amount of syllables each line requests.

Cinquain Poetry First Draft

1. **Topic** *(a 1-or-2 syllable word)*

2. **Adjectives Describing the Topic** *(4 syllables)*

3. ***-ing* Words Expressing the Actions of the Topic** *(6 syllables)*

4. **A Phrase with a Verb** *(8 syllables)*

5. **Synonym for Topic** *(a 1-or-2 syllable word)*

After writing your first draft, use your student forms to edit it.

Cinquain Student Forms
Checklist and Peer-Conferencing

I. Checklist

1. Look at your poem. Is it written in the correct format?
   ❑ Yes   ❑ No

2. Read your cinquain to yourself quietly. Does it make sense?
   ❑ Yes   ❑ No

3. Do you have the correct amount of syllables on each line?
   ❑ Yes   ❑ No

4. Did you use strong, clear, and descriptive words?
   ❑ Yes   ❑ No

II. Peer-Conferencing

Now, read your poem to another student, your peer-editor. Ask him or her to check "Yes" or "No" after the questions below.

1. Is the poem complete (five lines)?
   ❑ Yes   ❑ No

2. Does the poem have a nature theme?
   ❑ Yes   ❑ No

3. Does the writer follow the rules of the poem?
   ❑ Yes   ❑ No

4. Is the topic a noun?
   ❑ Yes   ❑ No

5. Are there descriptive adjectives?
   ❑ Yes   ❑ No

6. Are there words ending in -ing (participles)?
   ❑ Yes   ❑ No

7. Is the synonym at the end of the poem creative and appropriate?
   ❑ Yes   ❑ No

Attach this form and the next one to your first draft. You will need to refer to them as you complete your final draft.

Cinquain Student Forms *(cont.)*
Peer-Editing

III. Peer-Editing

Give your poem to your peer-editor. It is now the editor's responsibility to use a different colored pen to mark corrections directly onto the paper.

Note to the editor: Change grammar and punctuation errors with pen on the paper. However, if you think there is a spelling error, simply circle it. It is the author's responsibility to look up the word and correct the error.

1. Ideas are clear and understandable?
   ❑ Yes ❑ No

2. Spelling errors?
   ❑ Yes ❑ No

3. Punctuation errors?
   ❑ Yes ❑ No

4. Capitalization errors?
   ❑ Yes ❑ No

5. Appropriate amount of syllables in each line?
   ❑ Yes ❑ No

6. Is the handwriting legible?
   ❑ Yes ❑ No

Editor's compliments about this project: _____

_____

_____

_____

Editor's suggestions for improvement: _____

_____

_____

_____

Cinquain Reflection Sheet

1. My topic was_____.

2. Why did you choose this topic for your cinquain? _____

   _____

3. Which part of the cinquain did you enjoy doing the most and why? _____

   _____

4. What was the hardest part of this writing experience and why?_____

   _____

5. Did you try to use strong vocabulary words? _____

   _____

6. Write your best vocabulary choices below.

   _____   _____

   _____   _____

7. What was the synonym you wrote?_____

   Did it conclude your poem well? How effective was it? _____

   _____

8. If you had the opportunity to rewrite your poem what would you improve upon?

   _____

   _____

9. What content or mechanical errors did you discover while you were completing the
   student checklist?

   _____

10. How did your peer-conferencing session help you improve the cinquain?

    _____

    _____

    _____

    _____

Grade Sheets

Cinquain Grade Sheet

Name_____

Nature theme_____

Descriptive adjectives _____

Accurate participles _____

Synonyms _____

Neatness and form _____

Comments _____

_____

Rubric

Cinquain Grade Sheet

Name_____

Nature theme_____

Descriptive adjectives _____

Accurate participles _____

Synonyms _____

Neatness and form _____

Comments _____

_____

Rubric

Cinquain Grade Sheet

Name_____

Nature theme_____

Descriptive adjectives _____

Accurate participles _____

Synonyms _____

Neatness and form _____

Comments _____

_____

Rubric

Cinquain Grade Sheet

Name_____

Nature theme_____

Descriptive adjectives _____

Accurate participles _____

Synonyms _____

Neatness and form _____

Comments _____

_____

Rubric

Lesson Plan: The Holiday Mouse

Objectives   Students will write fictional stories, beginning with interesting story openers, or leads about an imaginary mouse.
Students will use personification to represent the mouse.
Students will correctly use quotation marks in at least six places in their stories.
Students will continue to refine and edit their stories based on peer-editing and peer-conferencing results.
Students will complete their final drafts on a computer.

Materials   copies of pages 70 –77

Introduction   Begin the lesson with a discussion about point of view. Ask your students to carefully stand on their chairs and look at their surroundings. Then ask them to sit on the floor and compare this perspective to the one they just had. This will help them to imagine the various views different types of animals have. Discuss the meaning of personification. The stories they will be writing will be told from the point of view of a mouse. Have them imagine that this mouse character is living in their houses during the holidays.

Directions   Direct your students to plan the characters and the events in their stories.

Assessment   Students will be graded on five aspects of this project.
    A. Use of point of view (the mouse character in first person)
    B. Use of a strong opener or "grabber"
    C. Use of personification
    D. Content of story
    E. Mechanics: capitalization, grammar, and use of quotations and punctuation

Rubric Scores: 3 = High pass   1 = Needs revision
                      2 = Moderate pass   0 = No response

	Mouse Story Rubric
3	Student responds to directions, creates a story with personification, demonstrates a strong story opener, uses correct mechanics, and completes the correct point of view.
2	Student responds to directions, creates a story with unclear personification, demonstrates an adequate story opener, uses mechanics which do not hinder understanding, completes incorrect point of view.
1	Student may not respond to directions, creates partial story without personification, demonstrates a weak story opener, uses mechanics which hinder understanding, completes incorrect point of view.
0	No response

Reassessment   Students will have the opportunity to rewrite their stories if they wish to improve their grades in specific skill areas.

Student Information Pages

Holiday Mouse Story Openers

Openers are introductions to a story which grab the attention of the reader and make them want to read more of the story. They are sometimes called "grabbers."

The following examples are excellent types of openers.

1. Standard

It was what we thought would be an ordinary day before Christmas. The whole family was decorating the house. Mom, Dad, my sister, and I had been decorating all day and my mom and I were hanging the stockings over the fireplace. It was the last task to finish before dinner. My dad and sister were putting the finishing touches on the wreath on the kitchen door. Suddenly we were all startled by a loud crash coming from the kitchen.

2. Action: A character doing something

I ran to the kitchen as fast as my legs could carry me on the slippery floor in the hallway, hurrying toward the loud crash that my mom and I had just heard from the kitchen.

"Brian!" my dad shouted to me. "Hurry! You're not going to believe this!"

"I'm coming!" I gasped as I pushed open the door to the kitchen.

3. Dialogue: A character or characters saying something

"Brian! Come in here on the double!" my father called from the kitchen.

"Dad?" I called back. "Where are you?" I was hanging our stockings over the fireplace with my mom. It was a few days before the holidays officially began.

"Brian, hurry! You're not going to believe this," dad's voice urged me. I dropped the stocking and rushed to the kitchen, pushing open the door.

4. Reaction: A character thinking about something

I could not imagine what my father could be shouting to me about from the kitchen. I thought hard and fast about what I might have done to make him so upset even on a night during the holidays. Maybe he had heard about the way I had spoken to my mother the night before when she had asked me to take out the trash. Before I could consider another possibility my dad's voice broke through my thoughts.

"Brian, hurry! You're not going to believe this!"

70

Student Information Pages *(cont.)*

Holiday House Dialogue Ideas and Speaker Verbs

This story is being written from the point of view of a mouse who might have lived in your home during the holidays. When you have the mouse speak and do other human-like activities it is called *personification*. You need to write at least six quotations, showing conversations in the story between family members and the mouse.

Quotation marks show where the speaker's words begin and end. Several rules are helpful when writing quotations.

Rules and Examples:

The first word of a quotation begins with a capital letter. A comma separates the quotation from the words that tell who is speaking.

"I think I just saw a giant," I said, as I poked my head out of my mouse hole.

Use an exclamation mark or question mark instead of a comma when writing a sentence with strong feeling.

"I think it would be fantastic!" I told the big kid with yellow hair when he suggested taking me to the kitchen for a quick breakfast.

Some quotations are divided. If a divided quotation is one sentence, use commas to separate the quotation from the speaker.

"I would love to go to the mall with you," I answered, "but I need to finish my chores first."

When you quote a person speaking, begin a new paragraph each time the speaker changes. Vary the speaker tags that you use.

"Does the large man in the hallway give out green paper to everyone who lives in this building?" I asked. "I don't think so," replied Jose.

To avoid using the word "said" over and over again, replace it where appropriate. Use the list of verbs below as speaker tags to replace the word "said."

added	cheered	explained	ordered	shuttered
admitted	chuckled	fretted	panted	sighed
answered	coaxed	gasped	pleaded	smiled
argued	confessed	greeted	praised	smirked
asked	corrected	hinted	prayed	snickered
babbled	cried	informed	promised	stammered
bawled	croaked	insisted	questioned	stated
bet	dared	laughed	quoted	suggested
blurted	decided	lied	ranted	tempted
bragged	declared	murmured	reminded	wailed
bugged	demanded	named	replied	wept
called	denied	nodded	requested	whispered
cautioned	ended	nudged	roared	wondered
chatted	exclaimed	offered	sassed	yelled

Student Planner

Planning The Holiday Mouse Story

Characters

1. Mouse name _____

2. _____

3. _____

4. _____

5. _____

Place-Setting

Plot

Introduce Mouse	Mouse Adventures	Discovered	What happens?
Beginning	**Middle**	**Climax**	**Conclusion**

Keep track of your quotations as you write them.

1_____   2_____   3_____   4_____   5_____   6_____

The Holiday Mouse Student Forms

Checklist and Peer-Conferencing

I. Checklist

1. Look at your story. Is it written in the correct format?
   ❑ Yes ❑ No

2. Read your mouse story over quietly to yourself. Does it make sense?
   ❑ Yes ❑ No

3. Have you said enough or do you need to add more detail or description?
   ❑ Yes ❑ No

4. Is your opener interesting?
   ❑ Yes ❑ No

5. Did you use at least six quotations?
   ❑ Yes ❑ No

II. Peer-Conferencing

Now, read your story to another student, your peer-editor. Ask him or her to check "Yes" or "No" after the questions below.

1. Is the opener interesting?
   ❑ Yes ❑ No

2. Is the story complete?
   ❑ Yes ❑ No

3. Are the characters well described?
   ❑ Yes ❑ No

4. Are the descriptions creative and appropriate?
   ❑ Yes ❑ No

5. Does the story have a clear setting?
   ❑ Yes ❑ No

6. Does the story have a logical and understandable ending?
   ❑ Yes ❑ No

7. Does the story have paragraphs which change with each new time, place, and speaker?
   ❑ Yes ❑ No

8. Is the story written from the point of view of a mouse?
   ❑ Yes ❑ No

9. Did the writer include six correct quotations?
   ❑ Yes ❑ No

10. Are the speaker tag verbs interesting and varied?
    ❑ Yes ❑ No

The Holiday Mouse Student Forms *(cont.)*
Peer-Editing

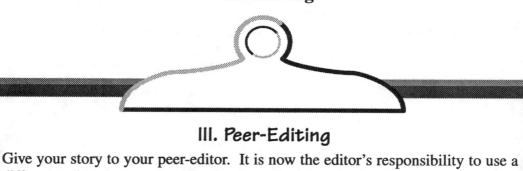

III. Peer-Editing

Give your story to your peer-editor. It is now the editor's responsibility to use a different colored pen to mark corrections directly onto the paper.

Note to the editor: Change grammar and punctuation errors with pen on the paper. However, if you think there is a spelling error, simply circle it. It is the author's responsibility to look up the word and correct the error.

1. Ideas are clear and understandable?
   ❏ Yes ❏ No

2. Spelling errors?
   ❏ Yes ❏ No

3. Punctuation errors?
   ❏ Yes ❏ No

4. Capitalization errors?
   ❏ Yes ❏ No

5. Paragraphs are indented?
   ❏ Yes ❏ No

6. Is the handwriting legible?
   ❏ Yes ❏ No

Editor's compliments about this project: _____

_____

_____

_____

Editor's suggestions for improvement: _____

_____

_____

_____

Attach these forms to your first draft. You will need to refer to them as you complete your final draft.

The Holiday Mouse Reflection Sheet

1. What skills did you learn while writing this fictional story?

   _____

   _____

   _____

2. Do you think that your opener (introduction) is strong and would make readers want to continue reading? Why or why not?

   _____

   _____

3. What is your favorite part of your story and why?

   _____

   _____

4. How did you involve the mouse character with the family characters?

   _____

   _____

   _____

5. What was the hardest part about writing this story?

   _____

   _____

6. What was the first dialog you wrote?

   _____

   _____

7. How did the inclusion of direct quotations from your characters, instead of just writing about them, enhance your story?

   _____

   _____

   _____

8. If you had the opportunity to rewrite your story what would you improve upon?

   _____

The Holiday Mouse Reflection Sheet *(cont.)*

9. When you read your story aloud, how did your editor help you improve your story?

_____

_____

_____

10. Who was your peer-editor? How did he or she help you with mechanical errors?

_____

_____

_____

11. If you were to write a sequel (or a part two) to your mouse story, what would it be about?

_____

_____

_____

_____

_____

_____

12. Write an attention-grabbing opener for a mouse story sequel.

_____

_____

_____

_____

_____

_____

Grade Sheets

Mouse Story Grade Sheet

Name _____

Interesting opener _____

Point of view _____

Personification _____

Content of story _____

Mechanics _____

Quotations _____

Comments _____

_____

Rubric

Mouse Story Grade Sheet

Name _____

Interesting opener _____

Point of view _____

Personification _____

Content of story _____

Mechanics _____

Quotations _____

Comments _____

_____

Rubric

Mouse Story Grade Sheet

Name _____

Interesting opener _____

Point of view _____

Personification _____

Content of story _____

Mechanics _____

Quotations _____

Comments _____

_____

Rubric

Mouse Story Grade Sheet

Name _____

Interesting opener _____

Point of view _____

Personification _____

Content of story _____

Mechanics _____

Quotations _____

Comments _____

_____

Rubric

Overview of Chocolate Picture and Chocolate Poem Lessons

The two projects starting on pages 79 and 82 coordinate with one another. You may choose to do either of them first, although this book describes the drawing activity before the poetry activity.

Chocolate Picture

This original idea came from a home decorating magazine in which the wife of rock star Ricky Nelson described an activity she had done with their children. This art activity also works well in the classroom. Your students will each draw three sketches of a candy bar. The first sketch will show the candy bar whole and wrapped. The second drawing will show the candy bar partially unwrapped with a bite missing. The final drawing will show the candy bar completely unwrapped and almost all eaten (this sketch should also include the wrapping and crumbs). These pictures will then be colored with markers, crayons, or colored pencils and glued on a long strip of brightly colored construction paper in consecutive order. (See the example at the bottom of this page.) This activity will lead into the second part of the project, writing a poem about chocolate.

Chocolate Poem

Discuss with your students some of the many different feelings and words that we associate with chocolate. Ask them to recall the tastes of their chocolate bars from the art activity. Encourage them to use this experience to stimulate chocolate adjectives. Then discuss rhythm and rhyme. Following these discussions ask the students to fill in their planners and then write their chocolate poems. If students do not want to use the form of poetry suggested, they may use any other forms they wish, as long as they utilize rhythm and rhyme.

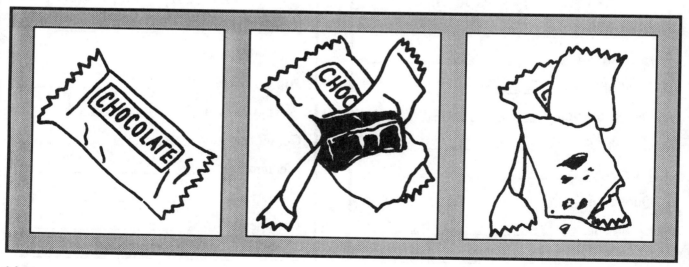

Note:

Before allowing any of your students to eat the chocolate bars used in the art activity, make sure that none of your students are allergic to chocolate or cannot have it for any other reason. If you do have any such students, allow them to do the activity using a lollipop, granola bar, banana, or any other food with a wrapper.

Lesson Plan: Chocolate Picture

Objectives   Students will each draw three pictures of their chocolate bars in the process of being eaten.
Students will plan the pictures in light pencil and then trace over the lines in ink.
Students will color in the drawings to match their original candy bars.
Students will complete their projects by gluing the pictures to background papers.

Materials   copies of pages 80 and 81, candy bars, brightly colored construction paper, white paper, glue, markers or colored pencils

Introduction   Begin the lesson by discussing the fact that many people love chocolate. Also discuss the marketing techniques the chocolate companies use to help sell their candy bars. Ask your students what they notice when in line at the grocery store. Discuss candy bar wrappers' colors and font styles.

Directions   Give each student a candy bar. (**Note:** You may ask your students to each bring in a candy bar of their choice. This will add diversity to the art pieces and keep costs down.) Direct your students to sketch these three pictures: a wrapped candy bar, a partially unwrapped candy bar with one bite missing, a completely unwrapped and mostly eaten candy bar (including crumbs and wrappers).

Explain that they will be the ones unwrapping and eating their candy bars. (**Warning:** See the note on the bottom of page 78.) When they are finished making their pencil sketches, have them go over their drawings in ink. Then, challenge them to color their drawings to replicate the original candies and wrappers. When the drawings are completed, glue them to long strips of brightly colored construction paper.

Assessment   Students will be graded on three aspects of this activity.

    A. Use of three pictures in consecutive stages

    B. Use of color

    C. Neatness of drawing, coloring, and gluing

Rubric Scores:	**3 = High pass**	**1 = Needs revision**
	2 = Moderate pass	**0 = No response**

Chocolate Picture Rubric	
3	Student responds to directions, draws three pictures of a chocolate bar being eaten, demonstrates ability to copy object accurately, uses color to show marketing appeal.
2	Student responds to directions, draws three partial pictures of a chocolate bar being eaten, demonstrates partial ability to copy object accurately, uses some color to show marketing appeal.
1	Student may not respond to directions, unclear pictures of a chocolate bar being eaten with little detail, demonstrates poor ability to copy object accurately, uses little color to show marketing appeal.
0	No response

Reassessment   Students will have the opportunity to rewrite projects if they wish to improve their grades in specific skill areas.

Chocolate Picture Reflection Sheet

1. Were you able to sketch your candy bar to your satisfaction? _____ Why or why not?

   _____

   _____

2. What did you learn while drawing the three pictures of your chocolate bar?

   _____

   _____

3. What words could you use to describe the tastes of the chocolate bar you ate?

   _____   _____   _____

   _____   _____   _____

4. What words could you use to describe the packaging of your candy bar?

   _____   _____   _____

   _____   _____   _____

5. Why do you think the wrapper of your candy bar was designed the way it was?

   _____

   _____

6. If you were in charge of marketing your candy bar how would you do it?

   a. Think of a new, catchy name. _____

   b. Design new packaging.

   ┌─────────────────────────────────────┐
   │   │
   │   │
   │   │
   │   │
   └─────────────────────────────────────┘

   c. Explain why you designed the wrapper the way you did. _____

   _____

7. What did you like best about your chocolate pictures?

   _____

Grade Sheets

Chocolate Picture Grade Sheet

Name_____

Three clear pictures of a candy bar
being eaten _____

Color and design_____

Neatness in drawing, coloring, and
gluing _____

Comments _____

_____

Rubric

Chocolate Picture Grade Sheet

Name_____

Three clear pictures of a candy bar
being eaten _____

Color and design_____

Neatness in drawing, coloring, and
gluing _____

Comments _____

_____

Rubric

Chocolate Picture Grade Sheet

Name_____

Three clear pictures of a candy bar
being eaten _____

Color and design_____

Neatness in drawing, coloring, and
gluing _____

Comments _____

_____

Rubric

Chocolate Picture Grade Sheet

Name_____

Three clear pictures of a candy bar
being eaten _____

Color and design_____

Neatness in drawing, coloring, and
gluing _____

Comments _____

_____

Rubric

Lesson Plan: Chocolate Poem

Objectives   Students will write poems about chocolate.

Students will use rhyming words and rhythm in their poems.

Students will continue to refine and edit their poems based on peer-editing and peer-conferencing sessions.

Students will complete a final draft, without mechanical errors, in ink or on computers.

Materials   copies of pages 83–88, pencils, erasable pens, markers or colored pencils

Introduction   Start by reviewing the chocolate art experience the students just finished. Ask them to describe the candy bars they ate. Consider such things as taste, texture, and smell when listing the chocolate adjectives. Discuss rhyme and rhythm and how they will be used in this activity. A good resource for rhyming words is *The Teacher's Book of Lists* (see bibliography). To further stimulate your students, read an excerpt from *Chocolate Fever*, by Richard Kimmel Smith, or *Chocolate Dreams*, by Arnold Adoff.

Directions   Direct your students to follow the Student Planner pages to write creative and delicious chocolate poems. After peer-editing and peer conferencing, have your students refine their poems for their final drafts.

Assessment   Students will be graded on four aspects of their chocolate poems.
   A. Use of chocolate theme
   B. Use of rhyme and rhythm
   C. Mechanics: capitalization, grammar, and punctuation
   D. Neatness

Rubric Scores: 3 = **High pass**   1 = **Needs revision**
                     2 = **Moderate pass**   0 = **No response**

	Chocolate Poem Rubric
3	Student responds to directions, writes a 16-line poem about chocolate, demonstrates correct use of rhyme and rhythm, uses a mastery of mechanics, grammar, and spelling.
2	Student responds to directions, writes a poem of moderate length about chocolate, demonstrates the partially correct usage of rhyme and rhythm, uses mechanics which enable the reader to understand the poem.
1	Student may not respond to directions, has unclear thoughts about the chocolate theme, demonstrates poor use of rhyme and rhythm, uses mechanics which inhibit the reader's understanding.
0	No response

Reassessment   Students will have the opportunity to rewrite their poems if they wish to improve their grades in specific skill areas.

Student Planner

Nearly everyone loves chocolate and writing about chocolate is almost as much fun as eating it. You will be writing a 16-line poem about chocolate. Try to rhyme the last words in every line or every other line. The rhythm of the two and four lines should match (the two and four lines are marked on the next page). Your knowledge, ideas, and feelings about chocolate should be included. Think about how chocolate makes you feel, how it tastes, and the physical characteristics of all its different forms (chocolate drinks, chocolate candy bars, etc.).

You will be graded on four aspects of your poem.

1. How well did you use the chocolate theme?

2. Did you use both rhyme and rhythm?

3. Did you correctly use capitalization, grammar, and punctuation?

4. Is your poem written neatly?

Before writing the first draft of your poem on page 84, take time to do some brainstorming. The lists you create will become helpful when you are ready to write.

Brainstorm adjectives which describe chocolate.

_____   _____   _____

_____   _____   _____

_____   _____   _____

_____   _____   _____

Brainstorm a list of rhyming words which might be useful in a poem about chocolate.

_____   _____   _____

_____   _____   _____

_____   _____   _____

_____   _____   _____

Student Planner *(cont.)*

It is time to write the first draft of your poem. Four of the lines have been started for you. If you wish to begin these lines in a different way, write your first draft on the back of this paper instead. Remember, no matter how you format your poem, lines two and four must have matching rhythms and you must try to put rhyming words at the end of every line or every other line.

Chocolate Poem

Chocolate, oh chocolate,_____

_____ *(two)*

_____

_____ *(four)*

Chocolate, oh chocolate,_____

_____ *(two)*

_____

_____ *(four)*

Chocolate, oh chocolate,_____

_____ *(two)*

_____

_____ *(four)*

Chocolate, oh chocolate,_____

_____ *(two)*

_____

_____ *(four)*

Chocolate Poem Student Forms
Checklist and Peer-Conferencing

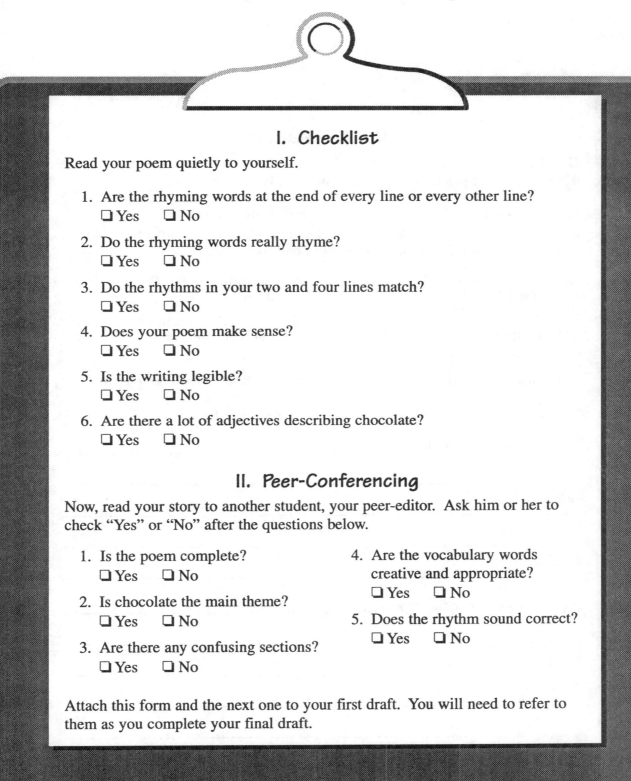

I. Checklist

Read your poem quietly to yourself.

1. Are the rhyming words at the end of every line or every other line?
   ❏ Yes   ❏ No

2. Do the rhyming words really rhyme?
   ❏ Yes   ❏ No

3. Do the rhythms in your two and four lines match?
   ❏ Yes   ❏ No

4. Does your poem make sense?
   ❏ Yes   ❏ No

5. Is the writing legible?
   ❏ Yes   ❏ No

6. Are there a lot of adjectives describing chocolate?
   ❏ Yes   ❏ No

II. Peer-Conferencing

Now, read your story to another student, your peer-editor. Ask him or her to check "Yes" or "No" after the questions below.

1. Is the poem complete?
   ❏ Yes   ❏ No

2. Is chocolate the main theme?
   ❏ Yes   ❏ No

3. Are there any confusing sections?
   ❏ Yes   ❏ No

4. Are the vocabulary words creative and appropriate?
   ❏ Yes   ❏ No

5. Does the rhythm sound correct?
   ❏ Yes   ❏ No

Attach this form and the next one to your first draft. You will need to refer to them as you complete your final draft.

Chocolate Poem Student Forms *(cont.)*

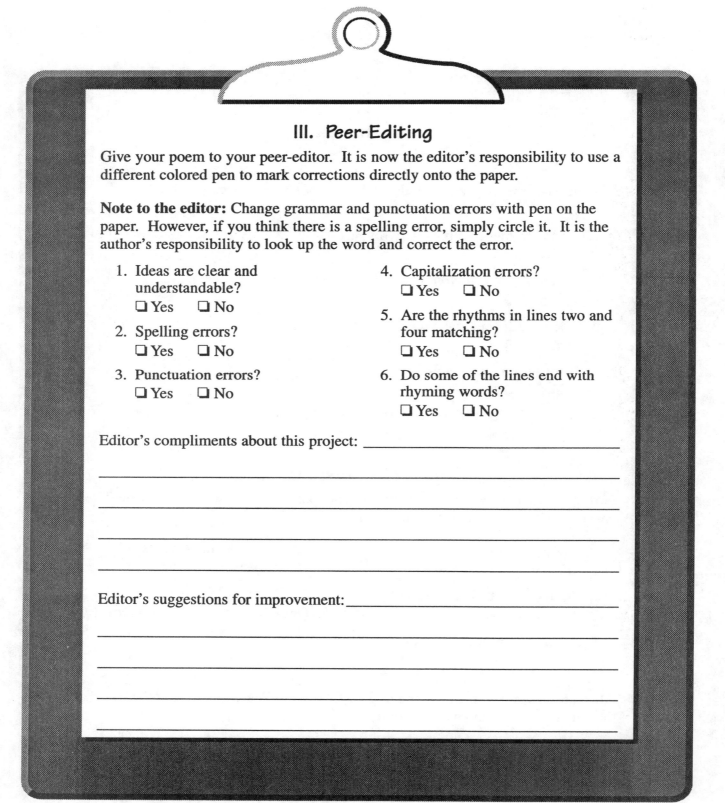

III. Peer-Editing

Give your poem to your peer-editor. It is now the editor's responsibility to use a different colored pen to mark corrections directly onto the paper.

Note to the editor: Change grammar and punctuation errors with pen on the paper. However, if you think there is a spelling error, simply circle it. It is the author's responsibility to look up the word and correct the error.

1. Ideas are clear and understandable?
   ❑ Yes ❑ No

2. Spelling errors?
   ❑ Yes ❑ No

3. Punctuation errors?
   ❑ Yes ❑ No

4. Capitalization errors?
   ❑ Yes ❑ No

5. Are the rhythms in lines two and four matching?
   ❑ Yes ❑ No

6. Do some of the lines end with rhyming words?
   ❑ Yes ❑ No

Editor's compliments about this project: _____

_____

_____

_____

_____

Editor's suggestions for improvement: _____

_____

_____

_____

_____

_____

86

Chocolate Poem Reflection Sheet

1. Do you feel that your poem accurately shows how you feel about chocolate? Explain why or why not.

   _____

   _____

   _____

2. How did your peer editor help you during your conferences?

   _____

   _____

3. Were you able to end every line or every other line with rhyming words?_____

4. What do you think were some of the strongest descriptive words you used?

   _____   _____

   _____   _____

   _____   _____

5. Where did you get your ideas for the chocolate poem?

   _____

   _____

6. What do you like best about your chocolate poem?

   _____

   _____

7. What was the hardest part about writing this poem?

   _____

8. If you were to use this same poetry format in the future, what themes (besides chocolate) would you like to write about?

   _____

9. If you had the opportunity to rewrite your chocolate poem, what would you improve upon?

   _____

   _____

Grade Sheets

Chocolate Poem Grade Sheet

Name_____

Use of rhyme_____

Chocolate theme _____

Use of rhythm_____

Mechanics _____

Comments _____

_____

Rubric

Chocolate Poem Grade Sheet

Name_____

Use of rhyme_____

Chocolate theme _____

Use of rhythm_____

Mechanics _____

Comments _____

_____

Rubric

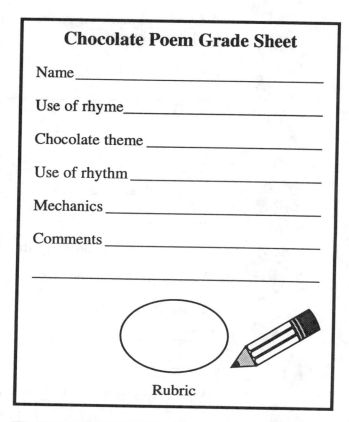

Chocolate Poem Grade Sheet

Name_____

Use of rhyme_____

Chocolate theme _____

Use of rhythm_____

Mechanics _____

Comments _____

_____

Rubric

Chocolate Poem Grade Sheet

Name_____

Use of rhyme_____

Chocolate theme _____

Use of rhythm_____

Mechanics _____

Comments _____

_____

Rubric

Lesson Plan: Persuasive Essay and Speech Project

Objectives   Students will write persuasive essays and then present speeches based on the essays. (Essay topics will be chosen by the students.)

Students will write five-paragraph essays, including introductions and conclusions.

Students will present their speeches in front of the class. (Speeches will be video taped.)

Students will reflect on their performances after viewing their taped speeches.

Materials   copies of pages 90–104, video tapes and a video camera, student-supplied visual aids

Introduction   Lead a discussion about persuasive writing and speech techniques. Then brainstorm a list of interesting speech and essay topics with your students.

Directions   Explain to your students that they will be writing persuasive essays. When they have finished writing their first drafts, they will hold peer-editing and peer-conferencing sessions. Next, they will write their final drafts to hand in. After the final drafts have been handed back to the students, they will begin to prepare their speeches. The Reflection Sheets will not be completed until after the speeches have been given.

Assessment   Student will be graded on several aspects of the persuasive essay and the speech.

      1. Essay
         a. Content   b. Mechanics   c. Organization
      2. Speech
         a. Delivery   b. Eye contact   c. Voice control and volume   d. Posture
         e. Visual aid

Rubric Scores: **3 = High pass**   **1 = Needs revision**
                  2 = Moderate pass   **0 = No response**

	Persuasive Essay Rubric
3	Student responds to the directions, creates a five-paragraph persuasive essay, demonstrates knowledge of subject, uses the correct mechanics.
2	Student responds to the directions, creates a four-paragraph persuasive essay, demonstrates partial knowledge of subject, uses mechanics that do not hinder understanding.
1	Student may not respond to directions, creates unclear paragraphs, demonstrates lack of knowledge of the subject, uses mechanics that hinder understanding.
0	No response

Reassessment   Students will have the opportunity to rewrite their projects if they wish to improve their grades in any of the specific areas of assessment.

Student Planner—Essay

You are about to write a persuasive essay, but before you get started, there are some things you should know about essay writing.

Rule Number One:

Never refer to the research paper itself.

Rule Number Two:

Never write that you are now going to tell about something.

Rule Number Three:

Never conclude with, "I hope you have enjoyed my essay."

Rule Number Four:

Never refer to the author (I) or the reader (you).

Example of what not to do:

In this research paper I am going to tell you about my topic.

Use strong action verbs in your essay. Some examples of action words are . . .

contribute	shape	lead
understand	continue	enjoy
influence	learn	learn
control	begin	compare
structure	discover	reflect
provide	import	establish

Some words and phrases you can use in listing examples and explaining are . . .

namely	for instance	in this way
to be specific	such as	
to explain	in particular	

Some words and phrases you can use in comparing are . . .

above all	as well as	furthermore
likewise	besides	
moreover	even more	

Some words and phrases you can use in contrasting are . . .

but	on the contrary	instead
nevertheless	in spite of	another

Some words and phrases you can use to conclude with are . . .

finally	it may be concluded	lastly

Keep this sheet for reference as you write your first draft.

Student Planner—Essay *(cont.)*

As your class brainstorms topics for the persuasive essay, write down some ideas that come to your mind.

1. _____   9. _____

2. _____   10. _____

3. _____   11. _____

4. _____   12. _____

5. _____   13. _____

6. _____   14. _____

7. _____   15. _____

8. _____   16. _____

Choose one of the essay topics from your list. Circle your choice.

Why did you choose this topic? _____

_____

_____

_____

_____

Before you begin writing, you should know that you will be graded on the content, mechanics, and organization of your essay.

Student Planner—Essay *(cont.)*

Use the web below to brainstorm ideas about the topic you have chosen. Write the topic and your point of view in the circle. On the lines, write as many ideas as you can think of to support that idea in the boxes. Also, try to add more lines onto your idea lines to include supporting details. You probably will not use everything that you write down, but the more you write while brainstorming, the easier it will be to write the first draft.

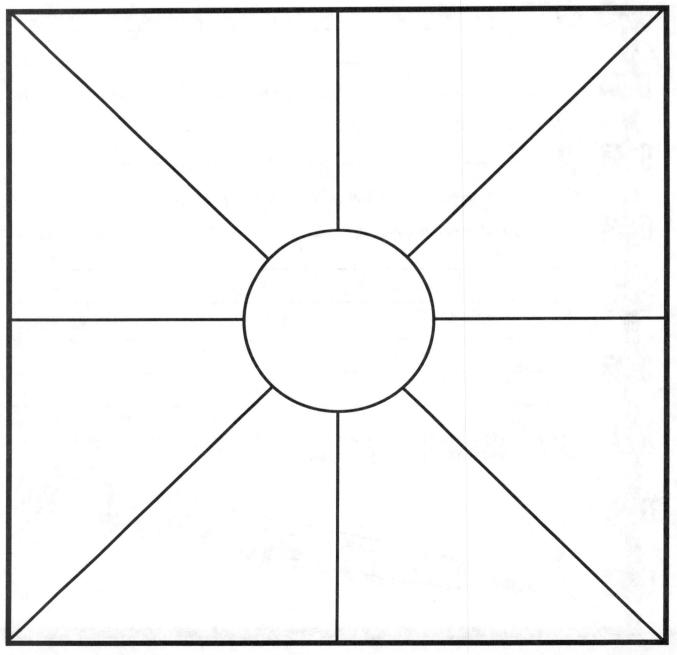

Student Planner—Essay *(cont.)*

Use the guidelines below to plan what you will write for the introductory paragraph of your essay.

First Sentence: The first sentence of your essay should be a quote, a question, or an attention-grabbing statement about your topic.

_____

_____

_____

Second Sentence: The second sentence of your essay should tell your opinion about the topic. This will be your main topic sentence or idea.

_____

_____

_____

Third Sentence: In the third sentence express clearly the three supportive arguments you will be discussing in the body of your essay.

> **Example:** Maddison School should use uniforms because they cost less money than other clothes, they usually look neat, and students would not be hassled for their clothes.

_____

_____

_____

Fourth/Transition Sentence: This sentence should connect the introduction paragraph to the body of the essay. Try to use a transition word or phrase from the word list on the first page of this Student Planner.

_____

_____

_____

Student Planner—Essay *(cont.)*

In the chart below, write and organize your ideas for paragraphs two through four.

Second Paragraph	Third Paragraph	Fourth Paragraph
First reason	Second reason	Third reason
Facts to support first reason	Facts to support second reason	Facts to support third reason
Examples of first reason	Examples of second reason	Examples of third reason

Student Planner—Essay *(cont.)*

Use the guidelines below to plan what you will write for the concluding paragraph of your essay.

First Sentence: The first sentence of your conclusion should be a transitional sentence from the body of the essay to the ending of the essay.

_____

_____

_____

Second Sentence: The second sentence should restate your opinion in a different way than in your introduction. Use different verbs.

_____

_____

_____

Third Sentence: The third sentence should restate the three reasons you feel strongly about your topic.

_____

_____

_____

Fourth Sentence: The fourth sentence should mention any additional ideas or facts which add strength to your point of view.

_____

_____

_____

Final Sentence: The final sentence of your conclusion should explain how your position could affect the quality of your life and society in general.

_____

_____

_____

Persuasive Essay Student Forms
Checklist and Peer-Conferencing

I. Checklist

Read your essay quietly to yourself.

Is it written in the correct format?
   ❏ Yes   ❏ No

List the first words in each sentence below.

_____   _____   _____

_____   _____   _____

_____   _____   _____

Did you repeat any of the same words over and over **again**? If you did, change some of those now.

Does your essay make sense?
   ❏ Yes   ❏ No

II. Peer-Conferencing

Now, read your essay to another student, your peer-editor. Ask him or her to check "Yes" or "No" after the questions below.

1. Is the essay complete?
   ❏ Yes   ❏ No

2. Are the main topic and point of view clear?
   ❏ Yes   ❏ No

3. Are there any confusing sections?
   ❏ Yes   ❏ No

4. Does the conclusion summarize the point of view?
   ❏ Yes   ❏ No

Attach this form and the next one to your first draft. You will need to refer to them as you complete your final draft.

Persuasive Essay Student Forms *(cont.)*
Peer-Editing

III. Peer-Editing

Give your essay to your peer-editor. It is now the editor's responsibility to use a different colored pen to mark corrections directly onto the paper.

Note to the editor: Change grammar and punctuation errors with pen on the paper. However, if you think there is a spelling error, simply circle it. It is the author's responsibility to look up the word and correct the error.

1. Ideas are clear and understandable?
   ❏ Yes   ❏ No

2. Spelling errors?
   ❏ Yes   ❏ No

3. Punctuation errors?
   ❏ Yes   ❏ No

4. Capitalization errors?
   ❏ Yes   ❏ No

5. Is the writing legible?
   ❏ Yes   ❏ No

6. Are there five paragraphs and are they indented?
   ❏ Yes   ❏ No

Editor's compliments about this project:_____

_____

_____

_____

_____

Editor's suggestions for improvement: _____

_____

_____

_____

_____

_____

Student Planner—Speech

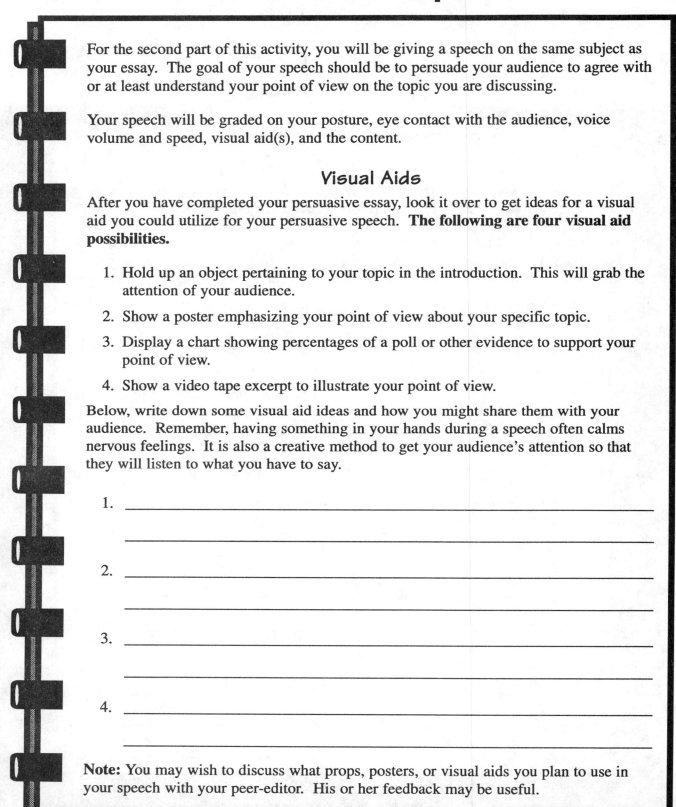

For the second part of this activity, you will be giving a speech on the same subject as your essay. The goal of your speech should be to persuade your audience to agree with or at least understand your point of view on the topic you are discussing.

Your speech will be graded on your posture, eye contact with the audience, voice volume and speed, visual aid(s), and the content.

Visual Aids

After you have completed your persuasive essay, look it over to get ideas for a visual aid you could utilize for your persuasive speech. **The following are four visual aid possibilities.**

1. Hold up an object pertaining to your topic in the introduction. This will grab the attention of your audience.

2. Show a poster emphasizing your point of view about your specific topic.

3. Display a chart showing percentages of a poll or other evidence to support your point of view.

4. Show a video tape excerpt to illustrate your point of view.

Below, write down some visual aid ideas and how you might share them with your audience. Remember, having something in your hands during a speech often calms nervous feelings. It is also a creative method to get your audience's attention so that they will listen to what you have to say.

1. _____

_____

2. _____

_____

3. _____

_____

4. _____

_____

Note: You may wish to discuss what props, posters, or visual aids you plan to use in your speech with your peer-editor. His or her feedback may be useful.

Persuasive Speech Student Forms

Checklist and Practice Sessions

I. Checklist

1. Did you read your speech quietly to yourself before performing it for your peer-editor?
   ❏ Yes   ❏ No

2. Did you practice your speech in front of a mirror, sister, brother, mother, father, friend, or neighbor?
   ❏ Yes   ❏ No

3. Did you practice your speech at least five times before the first peer-conferencing session?
   ❏ Yes   ❏ No

Suggestion: Try taping your speech on video or audio tape. Hearing (and seeing) yourself might help you perfect your speech.

II. Practice Sessions

Use this section to keep track of your practices and listeners' comments.

1. Date_____ Place_____ Listener_____
   Comments: _____

2. Date_____ Place_____ Listener_____
   Comments: _____

3. Date_____ Place_____ Listener_____
   Comments: _____

4. Date_____ Place_____ Listener_____
   Comments: _____

5. Date_____ Place_____ Listener_____
   Comments: _____

Persuasive Speech Student Forms *(cont.)*

Peer-Conferencing

III. Peer-Conferencing

Now, perform your speech for your peer-editor.

1. Does the speaker have good eye contact?
   ❑ Yes   ❑ No

2. Is the speaker's posture correct?
   ❑ Yes   ❑ No

3. Is the speaker's voice loud enough and at the right speed?
   ❑ Yes   ❑ No

4. Are you able to understand the speaker's words?
   ❑ Yes   ❑ No

5. Does the speaker have a good introduction?
   ❑ Yes   ❑ No

6. Does the speaker have at least one visual aid?
   ❑ Yes   ❑ No

7. Are the speaker's persuasive ideas strong?
   ❑ Yes   ❑ No

Editor's compliments about this project: _____

_____

_____

_____

Editor's suggestions for improvement: _____

_____

_____

_____

Reflection on Video or Audio Tape

This sheet should be filled out after listening to an audio tape or watching a video tape of your speech.

Topic of Speech _____

How did you prepare for your speech? _____

Rate yourself in the following areas: (Use the grades A, B, and C.)

Volume of Voice_____   **Knowledge of subject**_____

Rate of speed_____   **Posture**_____

Eye contact _____

1. What was your strongest area and why?

   _____

   _____

2. If you were given the opportunity to rewrite your speech, what would you change?

   _____

   _____

3. How did your body movement affect your speech?

   _____

   _____

4. What was your favorite part of the speech?

   _____

   _____

5. What type of visual aid did you use and how did it help you?

   _____

   _____

Reflection on Video or Audio Tape *(cont.)*

6. What did you dislike about giving the speech?

_____

_____

_____

7. What surprised you about watching your speech on tape?

_____

_____

_____

8. What was a good suggestion from your editor that you used in giving your speech?

_____

_____   **Photograph of Speech Day**

_____

_____

_____

_____

Grade Sheets

Essay Grade Sheet

Name _____

Content _____

Introduction _____

Body _____

Conclusion _____

Mechanics _____

Comments _____

Rubric

Essay Grade Sheet

Name _____

Content _____

Introduction _____

Body _____

Conclusion _____

Mechanics _____

Comments _____

Rubric

Essay Grade Sheet

Name _____

Content _____

Introduction _____

Body _____

Conclusion _____

Mechanics _____

Comments _____

Rubric

Essay Grade Sheet

Name _____

Content _____

Introduction _____

Body _____

Conclusion _____

Mechanics _____

Comments _____

Rubric

Grade Sheets *(cont.)*

Speech Grade Sheet

Name_____

Posture_____

Eye contact _____

Voice volume _____

Voice speed _____

Use of a visual aid _____

Speech content _____

Comments _____

_____

Rubric

Speech Grade Sheet

Name_____

Posture_____

Eye contact _____

Voice volume _____

Voice speed _____

Use of a visual aid _____

Speech content _____

Comments _____

_____

Rubric

Speech Grade Sheet

Name_____

Posture_____

Eye contact _____

Voice volume _____

Voice speed _____

Use of a visual aid _____

Speech content _____

Comments _____

_____

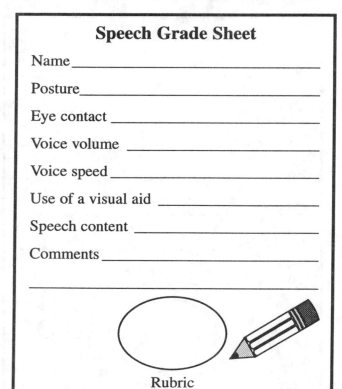

Rubric

Speech Grade Sheet

Name_____

Posture_____

Eye contact _____

Voice volume _____

Voice speed _____

Use of a visual aid _____

Speech content _____

Comments _____

_____

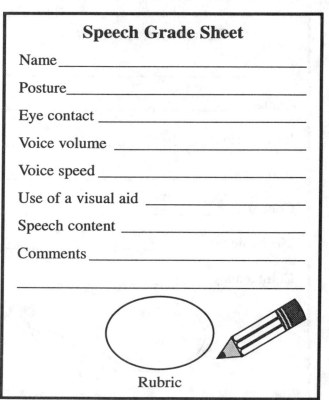

Rubric

End-of-the-Year Portfolio Reflection Sheet

Name _____

In my portfolio I am including work from my classes at _____

_____ School.

(Please list the projects you are including in your portfolio.)

1. _____

2. _____

3. _____

4. _____

5. _____

6. _____

7. _____

8. _____

9. _____

10. _____

Which one of these was your favorite piece of writing?

_____

How do you think this portfolio reflects you and your personality?

_____

_____

_____

If you had the opportunity to rewrite part of your portfolio, what part would you work on and why?

_____

_____

End-of-the-Year Portfolio Reflection *(cont.)*

What would you like to study further?

_____

What does your portfolio reveal about you as a writer?

_____

_____

_____

What does your portfolio tell about how you have developed as a writer this year?

_____

_____

_____

What strengths of yours does your portfolio indicate?

_____

_____

_____

What would you like to learn about next year?

_____

_____

_____

_____

What would you like your next year's teachers to know about you?

_____

_____

_____

_____

Peer-Committee Assessment of Portfolio

Get into a small group with several other students. Keep your group fairly small so that sharing all of your portfolios will not take too many group meetings. Allow each group member to present his or her portfolio to the group. This will be good practice for presenting your portfolio to a parent. Follow the presentation format below.

Committee Member Names

1. _____

2. _____

3. _____

4. _____

5. _____

Presentation Format

I am including work from my classes at _____ School.

(List five of your portfolio projects below.)

1. _____

2. _____

3. _____

4. _____

5. _____

My favorite piece of writing is _____ because

_____.

This is how I have organized my portfolio:_____

_____

Peer-Committee Assessment of Portfolio *(cont.)*

I feel that I have learned and/or improved many skills this year including:

(Here are some ideas, but do not limit yourself to just this list.)

brainstorming	rewriting	use of different genres
organization	improved spelling	speech presentation
peer-conferencing	improved punctuation	poetry
peer-editing	improved capitalization	fiction
revising	handwriting	non-fiction

My favorite form of writing was _____.

Why?_____

_____

_____

_____

My least favorite form of writing was _____.

Why?_____

_____

_____

_____

I would like to share an excerpt from a large project or an entire short project.

_____ (Share project with your group.)
              (Project Name)

In conclusion, I want to thank several people who have helped me become a better writer:

_____

_____

_____

_____

Peer-Committee Portfolio Grade Sheet

Fill out a copy of this grade sheet for each portfolio in your group. Be fair and honest and keep your comments confidential (this page is for you and the portfolio owner only). When you are finished, give your comments to the portfolio owner. You should receive one of these grade sheets back from each group member about your portfolio.

Portfolio Owner: _____ **Date:** _____

By reviewing this portfolio, what can you tell about its owner?_____

_____

_____

_____

_____

What do you believe are the strengths of this writer?

_____

_____

_____

_____

List two writing skills that you feel this author worked hard to improve upon this year.

_____

_____

Name one skill that this author needs to improve upon in the future.

_____

_____

_____
(signature of group member)

Grade Sheets

Portfolio Grade Sheet

Name _____

Well organized portfolio _____

Completed reflections for
each project _____

Portfolio shows development _____

Comments _____

_____

Rubric

Portfolio Grade Sheet

Name _____

Well organized portfolio _____

Completed reflections for
each project _____

Portfolio shows development _____

Comments _____

_____

Rubric

Portfolio Grade Sheet

Name _____

Well organized portfolio _____

Completed reflections for
each project _____

Portfolio shows development _____

Comments _____

_____

Rubric

Portfolio Grade Sheet

Name _____

Well organized portfolio _____

Completed reflections for
each project _____

Portfolio shows development _____

Comments _____

_____

Rubric

Parent Assessment of Student Portfolio

Dear Parent(s),

Please discuss your child's writing accomplishments of the year by reviewing his or her portfolio. Take the time to read some examples of your child's writing. Your child has selected each piece of writing to be shown, and it represents his or her personal best.

Please reflect on the portfolio by completing the rest of this page. Your child might choose to include this letter in his or her portfolio.

Date: _____

Dear _____ ,

After reviewing your portfolio, I think your writing strengths are _____

_____

_____

_____.

Personally, the thing I like the most in your portfolio is _____

_____

_____

_____.

Some writing goals we could set for the future are _____

_____

_____

_____.

_____
(parent's signature)

Bibliography and References

Bibliography

Atwell, N. *In the Middle.* Heinemann, 1987.

Cheeseman, Elaine. "Mark Twain Lives!" *Instructor,* pages 73–74, November/December, 1985.

Cooper, C.R. and Odell, (Eds.). *Evaluation Writing: Describing, Measuring, Judging,* (pages 128–134). National Council of English, 1977.

Graves, D. *Writing: Teachers and Children at Work.* Heinemann, 1983.

Gray, B. *Professional Handbook for the Language Arts.* Silver Burdett and Ginn, 1990.

Johns, J. *Literacy portfolios.* (Report No. CS 010 074) Northern Illinois University, 1990. (ERIC Document Reproduction Service No. ED 319 0200)

Krest, M. "Adapting the Portfolio to Meet Student Needs." *English Journal,* 79, pages 29–34, 1990.

Linek, W. M. "Grading and Evaluation Techniques for Whole Language Teachers." *Language Arts,* 68, pages 125–132, 1990.

Parkway School District. *Strategic Plan: A Report on the First Date (1989–1994).* Chesterfield, MO, 1990.

Shepard, L. "Why We Need Better Assessments." *Educational Leadership,* 46, pages 4–9, 1990.

Simmons, J. "Portfolios As Large-Scale Assessment." *Language Arts,* 67, pages 268–292, 1990.

Sudol, D. "Another Story: Putting Graves, Calkins, and Atwell in Practice and Perspective." *Language Arts,* 68, pages 292–300, 1991.

Vavrus, L. "Put Portfolios to the Test." *Instructor,* 68, pages 48–53, 1990.

References

Adoff, Arnold. *Chocolate Dreams.* Lothrop, Lee, and Shephard Books, 1989.

Daly, J. A. and M. D. Miller. "The Empirical Development of an Instrument to Measure Writing Apprehension." *Research in the Teaching of English,* pages 242–249, Winter 1975.

Fry, Edward B., Ph.D. *The New Reading Teacher's Book of Lists.* Prentice-Hall, 1985.

Madsen, Sheila. *The Teacher's Book of Lists.* Scott Foresman and Company, 1979.

Smith, Richard Kimmel. *Chocolate Fever.* Bantam Doubleday, 1972.